In His Grip

Foundations
for
Life & Golf

Quotations by E. M. Prain are from *Live Hands: A Key to Better Golf*, Portola Valley, Calif.: Warde Publishing, 1996.

J. Countryman is a registered trademark of Word Publishing, Inc.

A J. Countryman Book

Designed by: Koechel Peterson & Associates, Minneapolis, MN.

Photography credits:
Larry Lambrecht—cover (The European Club, 8th hole).
Clay Blackmore—endsheet.
Koechel Peterson & Associates—16/17, 18, 22, 28, 30, 33, 34, 42/43, 44, 46, 48, 51, 61, 67, 70, 74/75, 79, 80, 89, 92, 99, 102, 107, 109, 114/115, 119, 128.
Mark Feldman—21, 26, 39, 54, 58, 64, 73, 76, 83, 86, 94, 100/101, 110, 120, 122/123, 124.

Thanks to:
Nevada Bob's Golf, Bloomington, MN
Rush Creek Golf Club and Golf Academy, Maple Grove, MN

ISBN: 08499-5329-4

Printed and bound in Belgium.

In His Grip

By
Jim Sheard & Wally Armstrong

WORD PUBLISHING
Dallas • London • Vancouver • Melbourne

Table of Contents

Foreword
Tom Lehman

*Tom Lehman holding the Claret Jug
after winning the 125th British Open
in 1996 at Royal Lytham & St. Anne's*

It has always been my purpose to stay focused on my relationship with Jesus. I have never wanted my concentration on success as a tour pro to detract from the central place God has in my life. Nor do I want golf or whatever success I may achieve to become more important than my roles as husband and father.

Just as golf demands intense focus and concentration, so I have learned the importance of staying focused daily in God's Word. And my life would not be what it is today but for the time I spend in prayer each day— for me it has become as regular as breathing, an essential part of my life.

I want to encourage you to use these thoughts from Wally and Jim as a means to deepen your faith in God. I invite you to use this book to develop a closer relationship with him and his

Son, Jesus Christ, so that you may, in turn, share your faith with others.

As you read this book, I pray you will find the strength and courage you need from God to be his faithful follower. I also hope you will make it a point to be an encouragement to others—whoever they are, and wherever they may be in their Christian walk. I believe that both golf and the life of faith in Christ are exciting enough to share with any and all who want to listen.

I think I hear the starter calling us to the first tee.

Tom Lehman
July, 1997

A good drive puts Tom in position to win the 1996 British Open

A champion showing his skill around the green

Tom reads his putt at Royal Lytham & St. Anne's

A celebration of victory on the 18th green of the 1996 British Open

Preface
Jim Sheard & Wally Armstrong

Jim, Tom and Wally with Les Bostad—
legendary coach from the University of Minnesota

You don't have to look very far to realize that there's a frenzy out there to find the secret to the perfect golf swing. At the 1997 PGA show in Orlando, 1,300 exhibitors used one million square feet of space to display products and services for the golf consumer—much of it designed to help golfers hit the ball further and straighter, enjoy doing so, and look better doing it.

Many players assume there is some hidden secret that can be discovered in a club or putter design, teaching technique, or golf guru. They model their stance and strokes after their favorite player, read golf books and magazines, and pay close attention to the advertisements and endorsements featuring today's hot players and the legends of the past. They think they've finally found THE secret of the game—

at least for this week. But like most things in life, the true secret to playing the game well lies in *dedication* and *commitment*—a commitment to practice and to follow a proven plan based on truth and principle.

There is so much we can learn about life and golf by looking at parallels between the two. Life itself is like playing golf—every day is a new course with its twists and turns, and its ups and downs. In both, every shot counts. In life and golf we must plan ahead, learn from past experience, and prepare for future challenges. Golf and life involve recognizing our strengths and weaknesses, and being able to build on those strengths to overcome the weaknesses. As we learn to recognize the demands of both life and golf, we will need to determine what our response will be both to the obstacles and the opportunities.

In life, it is vital that we build a sure foundation of ethics and morality by which to live. If we don't have this solid moral footing, our lives will be established on little more

than shifting sand. Then, when the winds of challenge come—and they surely will come—you and I will be gripped by the turmoil of pressure, fear, anger, and failure. Golf, too, requires an unshakable foundation if we are to play by the rules and enjoy the traditions of the game.

This book will help you learn principles about golf and about life in God.

> *The true secret to playing the game well lies in dedication and commitment.*

Just as Jesus taught about everyday life using parallels and analogies in parables, so our goal is to take practical tips from the game of golf and tie them to eternal meanings. In this book we present information and lessons from the realm of golf, relate them to eternal truths in the Bible,

and encourage you to apply these truths in your own life.

Just as training aids in golf help you recognize and follow the right patterns or swing path, so the Word of God is a training aid for the game of life. It is "living and active, sharper than any two-edged sword . . . and discerning the thoughts and intentions of the heart" (Heb. 4:12). When you learn to understand and use God's Word, you will discover that it is a training aid of enormous value. In fact, you will discover it is the greatest training aid of all.

Dedicated golfers and athletes in all other sports recognize the need to warm up before practicing or playing. Yet, too few of us are in the habit of warming up before a round of golf. When we are not stretched out and limber, we become more prone to injury. We do not play as well as we could if we would simply take a few extra minutes to give our bodies a wake-up call that the game is about to begin.

The same is true in our walk with Christ. We all need to spend time each day warming up before we head out to face our various responsibilities as parents, spouses, employees, and friends. Our spiritual warm-up needs to include reading from God's Word and reflecting on its application for the day. This spiritual warm-up should also include prayer—a time when we praise God, ask for his forgiveness, and seek his help as our partner. It has been said that a person stands tallest when on his knees before God each day.

That is how we are to get ready to play the most difficult course of all . . . life!

This book will help you with your daily warm-up. It will give you ideas to help you draw closer to God. You will discover new, refreshing ways to walk with him, and to learn his wisdom for a more fulfilling life. At the same time, you may even improve your golf game as you apply time-tested truths and principles to your practice, playing, and attitudes about the game.

Here's to a great game—in God's grip.

Wally surveys his shot at Heathrow Country Club

Jim Sheard awaits a tee time at Town & Country Golf Club

Tom Lehman & Wally Armstrong sit down for a break at the 1994 President's Cup

James L. Sheard

Wally Armstrong

Jim Sheard
Wally Armstrong
June 1997

Jim escapes the Minnesota winter in sunny Florida

Introduction
Dr. Billy Graham

For many years I played golf. I enjoyed the game because it is so similar to the game of life, with its many obstacles, struggles, victories, conflicts, and blessings. If you're not modest about your abilities when you start playing the game, it won't take long for you to assume a role of humility—that's the nature of the game. Some people have suggested to me that golf is even mentioned in the Bible where the apostle Paul wrote, "I have fought a good fight, I have finished the course." However, I think that suggestion is definitely up for theological debate!

So what are some of the specific comparisons between golf and life? For one, in golf there is always the issue of the proper stance, whether the open stance, the straight stance, or the knock-kneed stance. I've seen some amateurs with an indescribable stance. But the stance dictates everything. In life, too, you and I will always assume some kind of stance—a stand for what we believe,

for how we'll live our life, and for what kind of legacy we'll want to leave behind.

I have found in golf that it's always been important to find a good leader—a coach—to help in understanding the correct fundamentals, and to be able to trust him with my total swing. This is similar to life in that we must trust our teacher, the Lord Jesus Christ, to help direct our lives and to make our lives abundant, worthwhile, and fruitful.

> *I enjoyed the game because it is so similar to the game of life.*

As an amateur golfer, I was always aware of the many different kinds of grips at my disposal. I was cross-handed in golf for many years and later switched over. In life, it is no different. We will *all* grip something, and we will all be *gripped* by something or someone. So my question to you is, Do you have a grip on your life? You may have a controlled backswing, but do you have control down inside? Your answer is critical to your success in the game of life.

When I was playing golf regularly, I was constantly hitting the ball from the outside. More than one pro told me that somehow I had to get that club on the inside of the line of flight. There may be some disagreement about that among professionals, but it certainly is true in life. We have to hit from the inside out. We have minds and bodies, and we develop them and try to keep them fit. But each of us also has a spirit, and yet, so many neglect it. The Bible teaches that "the world and the lust thereof shall pass away." It's all temporary. Only the one who does the will of God will abide.

One thing that's always been a challenge for me is keeping my eye on the ball. That's a cardinal rule in every sport, whether it's baseball, football, tennis, hockey, or golf. The New Testament speaks of "looking unto Jesus, the author and finisher of our faith." He is the one to whom we must give our undivided attention. He must be our focus. One of the most thrilling things in my life has been to keep looking to Jesus, to see what is really happening, to know where we are headed, and to have a reason for so much hope.

But not much matters in the game of golf if we don't follow the rules. Amateurs in golf often feel the rules are not fair. They don't like the idea of paying a penalty for breaking them. In like manner, God has laid down some rules in the Ten Commandments and in the Sermon on the Mount. At first glance, they may seem tough and unfair, but they were designed for our benefit. God says that if we live by them, we will find fulfillment and hope and relaxation and serenity even though the world may crumble around us.

Dr. Billy Graham & Arnold Palmer enjoy a round of golf with one another

I've had the privilege of speaking at the PGA Tour Bible studies numerous times, and it has been a thrill to see so many players stand up and share the excitement of their relationship with Jesus Christ. For any of us to grow in this relationship with our heavenly Father, it is of utmost importance that we have a consistent time with God, where we read his Word, and share with him our deepest thoughts, desires, and dreams. There's no substitute for a daily and weekly walk with God.

I believe this book, *In His Grip*, will be a tremendous opportunity for you to gain a better understanding of the game of golf. But more important, it will help you gain an appreciation for the importance of a deeper relationship with the Lord Jesus Christ. God wants to be your teacher, your coach. And if you will just give him your heart and your hands, he will guide you and direct your path.

Billy Graham

Billy Graham
June 1997

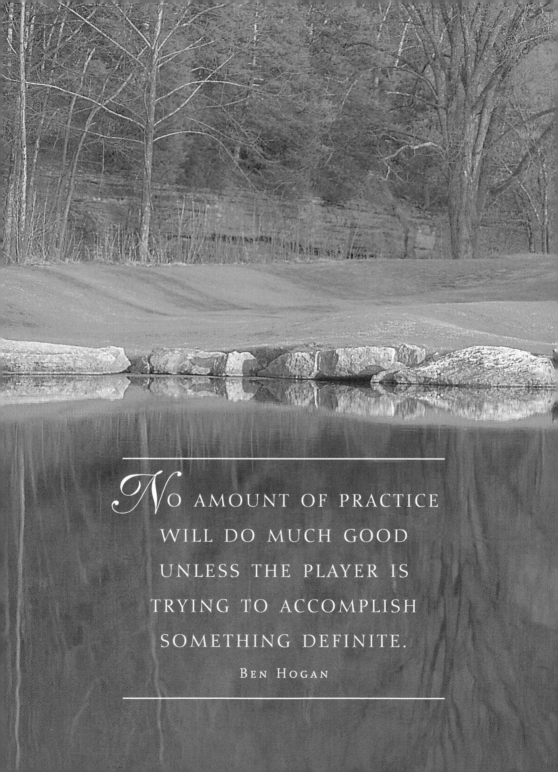

No AMOUNT OF PRACTICE
WILL DO MUCH GOOD
UNLESS THE PLAYER IS
TRYING TO ACCOMPLISH
SOMETHING DEFINITE.

BEN HOGAN

Living in God's Grip
Part One

In His Grip
Psalm 37:23–24

KEY VERSE

The steps of a good man are ordered by the LORD, and he delighteth in his way.
Though he fall, he shall not be utterly cast down:
for the LORD upholdeth him with his hand. (Ps. 37:23–24 KJV)

On January 30, 1996, Jim marked that passage from Psalms in his Bible and noted the date. Jim was two months into the most difficult year of his fifty-four years of life. Even with all the trappings of material success, his life was in shambles. No longer able to hold down his executive position due to clinical depression, he sought answers to life's most challenging questions: *What is the meaning of it all? Why has God not allowed me to fulfill the career he gave me? How will I provide for my family, find health insurance, have enough money for retirement? How can I enjoy golf if I don't even have the energy to walk eighteen holes? What am I to do with these intense emotions and feelings that keep invading my mind and body? How do I relate to my family and friends?*

Exactly one year later, Jim came to this Psalm in his Bible again. That's when he realized it was God alone who had sustained him during that difficult time. Jim realized more clearly than ever that he had been *in God's grip.*

Today, when the course of life is tough for you, when the "bunkers" at work or with your family seem impossibly high, when you don't know if you'll make the "green" in regulation, and when it seems there are few answers from a God who seems distant, rest assured there is a God who cares enough to hold you in his grip.

SWING THOUGHT

Thank God even for the obstacles in your path—those ever-present "bunkers." They will help you learn patience and make you aware of God's faithfulness.

19

Be Strong and Courageous
Joshua 1:5–9

KEY VERSE

Have I not commanded you? Be strong and of good courage; be not frightened,
neither be dismayed, for the LORD your God is with you wherever you go. (Josh. 1:9)

As Tom Lehman prepared for the final round of the 1996 U.S. Open at Oakland Hills in Birmingham, Michigan, he read Joshua 1:9, which speaks of being strong and courageous. This passage of Scripture was just the inspiration he needed for the final round in which he paired with his friend, Steve Jones.

As Tom and Steve walked down the first fairway, they prayed and spoke about truths they had learned from passages in Joshua. They reminded themselves of God's promise in verse eight, ". . . for then you shall make your way prosperous, and then you shall have good success." This verse was what they needed throughout the day as they battled the challenges and pressures that only the final round of a major can bring.

Although they were competing against each other for the U.S. Open title, when Steve hit his tee shot into the woods on the sixteenth hole, Tom encouraged him by reminding him that, "The Lord wants us to be strong and courageous." For Tom it would have been easy to see this as an opportunity to prevail against his friend rather than to encourage him. For Steve it would have been easy to falter, but instead he persevered and did not become discouraged. Although Steve won the U.S. Open title that day, both men experienced God's encouragement.

From this experience Tom and Steve were reminded that they didn't need to be frightened or dismayed because strength and courage *could* be theirs— if they continually went to the right source. While God promises to make our way prosperous and successful, it does not mean we will win every championship or succeed in every situation. It's that way in golf, and it's that way in life.

SWING THOUGHT

Regardless what pressures and challenges you face today, remember that God knows your name. He cares about you and wants to give you his strength and courage. He also wants you to be an encouragement to others.

Abounding in Hope
Romans 15:1–13

KEY VERSE

*May the God of hope fill you with all joy and peace in believing, so that
by the power of the Holy Spirit you may abound in hope.* (Rom. 15:13)

The headline of the *Golfweek,*
June 22, 1996, reads
"*Hallelujah! Jones completes
comeback with U.S. Open victory.*" The
cover photo shows Steve Jones
with his arms raised high in the air,
his putter in his right hand. He is
obviously shouting for joy just like
the caption says: "Steve Jones rejoices
after paring the 72nd hole and
winning his first major title."

The article relates what a long shot it
was for Steve to win the tournament.
He had not won since 1989 and hadn't
finished better than fourth since 1991.
He was 100th in the worldwide Sony
rankings and had missed three
seasons due to a finger injury in a
dirt bike accident. For a while, Steve
and others wondered if he would
ever play again.

Hallelujah was the right word for that
headline. A combination of two Greek
words for "praise" and "Jehovah," it
literally means "Praise the Lord"—
Steve's exact words following his
great victory. In fact, when you look
at the photograph of Steve after his
win, you can almost see the word
"hallelujah" jump off the page. He felt
that much joy.

Hallelujah is a word we can all use to
express our gratitude to God for all
his marvelous works in our lives.

SWING THOUGHT

Hallelujah! *To God be the glory for
the courage, stability, and peace he
gives us during our most difficult times.*

IF THE MIND CAN'T SEE IT
THE BODY CAN'T ACHIEVE IT.

WALLY ARMSTRONG

If the Lord Permits
1 Corinthians 16:4–9

KEY VERSE

For I do not want to see you now just in passing;
I hope to spend some time with you, if the Lord permits. (1 Cor. 16:7)

While the television audience saw Tom Lehman's name being engraved on the coveted Claret Jug, they did not see the actual presentation of the trophy for his winning the 1996 British Open. When Tom spoke to the assembled members of Royal Lytham & St. Anne's, accepting the Claret Jug, he said, *I just want to thank God for giving me this opportunity today to play in this tournament—to win this tournament. I really believe that God loves all of us. He has a special plan for our lives. Fortunately for me, today, it was in his plan for me to win. I know He cares about me. I know He cares about you. God bless you all. Thank you very much.*

God truly does have a plan for our lives—just as God had a plan for Tom to win that day. That is why we do well to hear the words of the apostle Paul who says he will spend time in Macedonia, "if the Lord permits." We have plans, but God directs our steps. With God as our source of strength, we can be focused on our goals and at the same time be spiritually flexible.

The first thing we must do is *make our first priorities* (verses 4–5) consistent with God's priorities. Then we are free to make detailed *flexible commitments* (verses 6–7) . . . as he permits. We can trust in *God's provision* (verse 6) and adapt to the practical flow of life (verse 8) as circumstances allow. The result of our faithfulness will be fruitful fields with wide open doors, even though there will always be *frustrating foes* who will oppose God's work in our lives (verse 9).

What happens to us on the golf course—and in all of life—is under God's control. Our job is simply to do our best and trust him for the results.

SWING THOUGHT

Be on the lookout for fruitful fields in your life. At the same time, be aware of frustrating foes who might throw up roadblocks and try to keep you from being your best for God. Remember, he is at work in your life.

Perseverance
Philippians 4:11–13

KEY VERSE
I can do all things in him who strengthens me. (Phil. 4:13)

An advertisement for Taylor Made™ described Tom Lehman as "dedicated, humble, and persevering." That's truth in advertising! That's the man he really is.

When testifying of his faith in Christ, Tom says he believes God has given him the strength to endure. He has played golf longer and spent more time on the so-called mini-tours than most of his competitors.

When it might have been easy to give up and take the coaching job at Minnesota, Tom and his wife Melissa sensed that God wanted him to persevere in playing golf. It was a difficult decision, and there were days when they wondered if they'd be able to pay their bills. But Tom *did* persevere,

and it paid off when he was named PGA Player of the Year in 1996 after winning the British Open. That year he was the top money winner on the tour and was rated second in the worldwide Sony rankings.

Philippians 4:11–13 describes the kind of perseverance that we should all want as our hallmark for living. Paul says we can do all things that are in God's will if we allow him to be our strength. That is how we, like Paul, will learn to face *plenty and hunger, abundance and want.*

Scott Simpson once said, "I want the same discipline in my faith that I have in my golf game." So it should be with you and me. We need both discipline and perseverance, and God will help us in our pursuit of both.

SWING THOUGHT

Today, ask God to keep you disciplined in your faith. And pray for his strength and power to help you persevere in all things.

The Confidence to Win
Proverbs 3:21–35

KEY VERSE
The LORD will be your confidence. . . . (Prov. 3:26)

When severe rains caused the delay of the 1996 Players Championship in Tulsa, Tom Lehman led the tournament by nine strokes. If the washed-out course couldn't be prepared for play on Monday, Tom would win the tournament, the money, and the scoring titles for 1996 without even playing the final round.

But Tom wanted the opportunity to play the full seventy-two holes to win the Players' Tournament—and the other titles that would be his by virtue of this win. He wanted to win without the asterisk of *only 54 holes played* stamped in his mind and in the minds of others. He also wanted to demonstrate that he had the confidence and ability to prevail.

Tom says one of the greatest lessons he has learned while struggling to make a living on the tour has been one of confidence in his ability to win. He says there was very little difference in his ability to play back in the 1980's, but he had not learned to play with confidence, to trust his ability. Through the years, as circumstances set up roadblocks to his goals and dreams—like the bad bounce into the fairway bunker on the 18th hole of the 1996 U.S. Open—Tom gained the confidence to fight back and to overcome the challenges that are part of the game of golf, and of life itself.

Without God as his source of strength and courage, it is unlikely Tom would have developed that confidence. God has gifted Tom with the ability to play the game of golf and has helped him gain the confidence he needs to win.

SWING THOUGHT

Winning in life requires a confidence that comes only from God—from understanding what he wants us to do and accepting his strength (ability) and his courage (willpower) to do it. The result? We become successful in what he sees as significant.

Purpose and Direction for Life

Part Two

Success or Significance
Hebrews 4:11–12

KEY VERSE

*For the word of God is living and active, sharper than any two-edged sword,
piercing to the division of soul and spirit, of joints and marrow,
and discerning the thoughts and intentions of the heart.* (Heb. 4:12)

Success lies in what we *do*. Significance lies in who we *are*. This critical difference challenges those of us who have grown up in a culture that rewards individuals more for what they do than for who they are.

Just about every worldly measure of success is based on what you can accomplish—on how much money you make, the kind of house you live in, the car you drive, how quickly you climb the corporate ladder . . . and the list goes on. But it doesn't stop there. Somehow we convey these same ideals to our children in the sports they play, the recreational activities they compete in, and even in the musical and academic contests they enter.

No question about it. We are an accomplishment-oriented society. Doing great things wins the prizes; *being* a person of significance often takes a back seat. In golf we are no different. Amateurs are judged by their handicaps. We judge tour players by their Sony ranking, career, current year earnings, number of majors won, and top ten finishes in a given year.

Don't we have this all backward? God certainly thinks so. He never measures us by what we *do* for him but by what we *are* for him—the character of our inner being.

Is it important what you *do*? Yes, it is. But it is far more important who you *are*—and far more difficult to measure. It is certainly not as easy as determining your handicap, average driving distance, or score for today's round, because it is a measurement of your heart.

SWING THOUGHT

Would you like to learn to evaluate yourself and others as God does? Ask him to help you concentrate on being rather than doing. Be assured that he will give you the strength and patience to know that as you do this, you are on the right track.

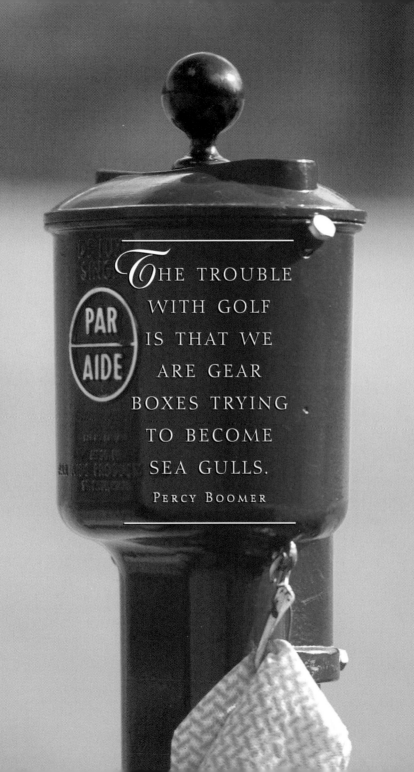

THE TROUBLE
WITH GOLF
IS THAT WE
ARE GEAR
BOXES TRYING
TO BECOME
SEA GULLS.

Percy Boomer

Your Chapter in the Book
1 Corinthians 3:10–15

KEY VERSE

Now if anyone builds on the foundation with gold, silver, precious stones, wood, hay, straw—each man's work will become manifest; for the Day will disclose it, because it will be revealed with fire, and the fire will test what sort of work each one has done. (1 Cor. 3:12–13)

During the 1996 U. S. Open, one telecaster made a comment that has been said many times in many different ways. The comment referred to Jack Nicklaus and the "big" chapter he has written in the book of golf.

People often speak of what a great man Jack is both on and off the golf course. His achievements are amazing, especially his wins at twenty-two major tournaments. Yet, through it all, he has never lost the desire to do well in everything he pursues, regardless of the number of trophies and awards he has already received.

It brings to mind an important question: When the "book" of your life is finally written, what will it look like? Will it be a chapter, a paragraph, or will it just be merely a sentence or two? What will be included, or excluded?

Have you done anything of eternal value? Will those who chronicle your life see a difference between your significance and your success? What have you done in life that is worth placing in the recorded annals of time?

We may have a track record that rivals Jack Nicklaus, yet still have nothing of significance to write about. On the other hand, though we may never achieve worldly fame we can still live lives of great significance, because what we do under God's control and direction is always significant.

SWING THOUGHT

What are the "majors" that God has called you to "win" in your life? What do you want your "chapter" to include? Is there anything you prefer that the writer leave out?

A Life of Learning
Colossians 1:9–14

KEY VERSE

We have not ceased . . . asking God to fill you with the knowledge of his will through all spiritual wisdom and understanding. (Col. 1:9)

A 1996 television commercial for the United States Golf Association asked the question "Why is it that we learn so much about ourselves on the golf course?" Good question. The commercial goes on to give some answers to this question. Each answer starts with the phrase "Perhaps it is because . . ."

We've written this book because we can learn so much about ourselves from the game of golf. This includes knowledge about our body, mind, and spirit.

Golf has characteristics that make it more than just another game. Some are devoted to it; some are addicted. No two golfers are alike, just as no two golf courses are alike, and no set of

circumstances will ever be the same in two rounds of golf. That's why the opportunities for learning the game are so enormous. It will never be the same from one round to another.

Our love for the game of golf also gives us a great opportunity to study ourselves, and to grow in our knowledge of the person of Jesus Christ. Of course there will be times of discouragement. But we know a faithful God will give us the strength to press on. There will also be occasions for celebration and great joy—when it all seems to be coming together. Both extremes are part of the game and part of our lives.

SWING THOUGHT

Lord, on and off the golf course, give me the wisdom to learn more about myself as I focus on you. I pray that you will give me the strength I need to make it through the peaks and valleys as I become the person you created me to be.

Today's Preparation—Tomorrow's Performance
Isaiah 40:28–31

KEY VERSE

They who wait for the LORD shall renew their strength, they shall mount up with wings like eagles, they shall run and not be weary, they shall walk and not faint. (Isa. 40:31)

In an article on patience in *Golf Illustrated*, Bobby Clampett states that his motto in 1983 as he returned to the British Open was "today's preparation is tomorrow's performance." He did not want to let the championship slip through his fingers again. His goal was to succeed through preparation for performance.

Bobby's preparation began weeks before the tournament was to be played at Royal Birkdale. Arriving with his caddie several days early, he struggled to get his swing into the "elusive groove."

His work ethic cranked up to playing two balls for twenty-seven holes per day, and then spending three to four hours in practice. This was in spite of calloused hands that needed clipping each night, and being almost too tired to rest. Still, he says the motto rang through his ears again and again— *"Today's preparation is tomorrow's performance."*

Bobby has learned what each of us need to learn. Just going through the trials of life does not guarantee us more patience. He says "The longest-lasting patience comes from having a well-defined purpose for existence, a reason for being, and an ultimate goal in life."

By preparing wisely today, we can have comfort and patience for tomorrow's performance. Preparation will usually make tomorrow's performance better. But even if tomorrow does not turn out as well as we had hoped, we can still know that God will sustain us in this effort if we wait on him. He will renew our strength, help us become like eagles, and cause us not to become weary or faint.

SWING THOUGHT

It's God's promise to you: today's preparation and the renewing strength of your heavenly Father will give you the performance of an eagle for tomorrow.

Find Your Game
Romans 12:3–8

KEY VERSE
Having gifts that differ according to the grace given to us, let us use them. (Rom. 12:6)

An advertisement for the Taylor Burner Bubble boldly reads "Find Your Game." One version of the ad says that Lee Janzen, despite his prior success, had never been able to "crack the top ten in driving distance" on the tour until he began to use the Burner Bubble driver.

With the increasing variety and of equipment available to golfers, a key is to find the equipment that best suits one's uniqueness as a player and as a striker of the golf ball. In shafts alone there is tremendous variety of materials, flexes, and kickpoints. The bubble shaft is one of the many potential "solutions."

In God's kingdom we are his workmanship and his tools. Each person is unique in design and skills. It is the obligation of each of us to understand how we have been shaped and gifted for his service. We must "find our game" of service for the Lord based on our own gifts and abilities for service in his kingdom.

This passage in Romans lists some specific ways God has equipped individuals with the gifts of the Holy Spirit. Other lists are found in 1 Corinthians 12:8–10, and 28; and Ephesians 4:11.

SWING THOUGHT

*In golf, to "find your game" means to learn to play the best you can within your unique set of capabilities and with the most complimentary equipment.
In life it means to find out how God has uniquely designed and gifted you for service in his kingdom.*

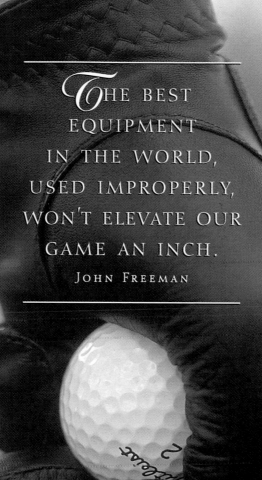

THE BEST
EQUIPMENT
IN THE WORLD,
USED IMPROPERLY,
WON'T ELEVATE OUR
GAME AN INCH.

JOHN FREEMAN

Preparation
for the Course
Part Three

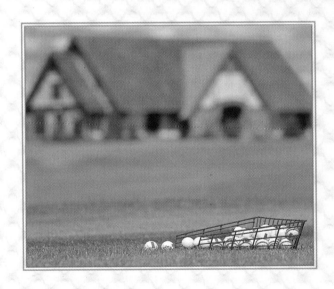

See Your Teacher
Isaiah 30:18–22

KEY VERSE

*Yet your eyes shall see your Teacher. And your ears shall hear a word behind you, saying
"This is the way, walk in it," when you turn to the right or when you turn to the left. (Isa. 30:20–21)*

This passage speaks of a Teacher who will show us the way to go forward. His guidance will be like words in our mind telling us how to move to the right or the left. The Teacher is God himself.

God is reminding us that while we will not be spared from affliction, he will not hide it from us. That's good news. He promises to be an encouragement to us—a faithful guide—if we but repent from our choice of following other gods and "images." This is a God who will be gracious to the sound of our cry for help and will answer us. (verse 19)

If you've ever needed serious help from a golf professional to fix your ailing golf swing, you can relate to this passage. And you *do* turn to a professional and not take advice from just anyone standing near the tee. You wouldn't dare trust your dilemma to anyone who didn't understand, who refused to be sympathetic to your need, or who would not be capable of giving you sound counsel on the way to resolve your dilemma.

That's the kind of a God we have available to us. We can call upon him, and he will guide us to the right or to the left with understanding and care. He is familiar with us and with our special needs. He alone must be our instructor in life, just as a pro must be present if we are serious about needing help with our golf swing.

> ## SWING THOUGHT
>
> *Learning to trust a golf instructor is like learning to trust God for his instruction. If you mess around without lessons for too long, the game of your life will show the results. But once you get the help you need, it's a different story. Are you ready to start working with the Pro for your life?*

Select Your Teacher
Matthew 23:1–11

KEY VERSE

But you are not to be called rabbi, for you have one teacher [Christ], and you are all brethren. (Matt. 23:8)

Virtually every golfer we know desperately wants to improve his game, but still only 8 percent of the golfers in America have had a single lesson from an instructor. Why this is true remains a puzzle. Perhaps most golfers simply don't realize the potential for improvement that could come from spending time on the practice tees with a qualified instructor. Others just may not know where to go for help.

For those who want instruction, the selection of an instructor is a key decision. If that person is you, then you want someone who can really help you, who'll be available, and whose price will not be prohibitive. You especially want to be sure your teacher will *help* rather than *hinder* your game.

What about the even bigger decision of deciding with whom you will spend eternity? Into whose hands will you put your trust for *this* event? Remarkably, some people think less about who is their God than who will be their golf instructor. The teacher for your life must also be trustworthy. He must have helped others and be capable of helping you throughout your life. His instruction should be supported by written documentation of who he is, what he teaches, what he expects of you, and what he promises. The only teacher that qualifies for this top position are the persons of the Trinity: God the Father, Son, and Holy Spirit—Teachers who will give you truth, eternal life, and an abundant journey of peace and joy.

SWING THOUGHT

There is no other teacher like the Trinity of God the Father, the Son, and the Holy Spirit. Each, in his own way is there to guide, instruct, and correct the "swings" of your life.

Habit Formation
Colossians 2:6–7; 4:2–6

KEY VERSE

As you therefore have received Christ Jesus the Lord, continue to live your lives in him, rooted and built up in him and established in the faith. (Col. 2:6–7)

When we first try to learn to do something it usually feels uncomfortable. We may try it once and then never attempt it again. That's because there are usually more forces working against us than for us. These include ease, comfort, and built-in reinforcement for a habit.

This means that forming a new habit in golf requires focused attention. It means we need to find a way for our mind and muscles to perform the new behavior properly, and then repeat it correctly. In other words, we need to practice the proper, rather than improper, behavior pattern—and we need to keep repeating it until it becomes as natural as breathing. Training aids, proper instruction, video feedback, and good coaching can all help to establish these good habits for the golf swing.

Habit formation in our spiritual journey with God is similar in many respects. It may be difficult to establish good habits such as spending regular time in God's Word and in prayer. It may be difficult to learn to practice the presence of God in the routine of our daily life. The process of developing these and other habits is called the "renewing of our life" or the "renewing of our mind." It's a process of ongoing spiritual growth, aided by the Holy Spirit through an understanding of God's word, by the encouragement of sound biblical teaching and preaching, and relationships within the Body of Christ.

SWING THOUGHT

Habit formation in golf and the renewing of our mind in Christ are both enhanced by solid teaching, devotion, commitment, and the encouragement of others. Make sure all these components are part of your game of golf, and your game of life.

Keep a Journal
Psalm 19:7–14

KEY VERSE

*Let the words of my mouth and the meditation of my heart be acceptable in thy sight,
O LORD, my rock and my redeemer. (Ps. 19:14)*

There is an untapped source of information available to people for improving their golf game and life. Isn't it amazing that we search everywhere for ways to improve in golf, and yet we search for answers to issues in our own life without looking to our most readily available resource—our own life's experience. The value of our own experience is typically lost to us because we don't have the discipline or take the time to draw on that experience. We also do not know how to record and utilize the available information.

SWING THOUGHT

Tap into the treasure of your own experience with a journal for your golf game and for your time with God. You'll not only see your daily progress, but you'll also see how God speaks to you in special ways. Your journal will become the most valued book in your entire library. Today would be a good day to make your first entry.

A few serious golfers have learned to record, track, and review information from each round of golf. This includes the more obvious information such as score, putts, fairways hit, greens in regulation, and sand saves. It might also include more detailed information on length of drives, miss-hits, swing thoughts, etc. These notes can be recorded in a notebook.

In our life, and in our time spent with God in prayer and quiet, this record-keeping process is called a prayer journal or simply a journal. It's a private place to record the names of people and occasions we want to pray for: pastors, missionaries, special prayer requests (yes, for a better golf game!) and other topics God has impressed upon us. One of those special items might be prayer for those who do not yet know the Savior. The journal is a place to record insights and thoughts that apply to each day and to our life in general. It's also a wonderful record of our life.

*M*OST GOLFERS
PREPARE FOR DISASTER.
A GOOD GOLFER
PREPARES FOR SUCCESS.

BOB TOSKI

Training Aids
Psalm 119:11–16

KEY VERSE

Your word I have hidden in my heart, that I might not sin against you. (Ps. 119:11)

Training aids are any devices that are helpful in learning new skills or concepts. They may help present the material or assist the learner in practicing and acquiring new or improved skills.

Training aids for the golf swing include a wide variety of devices that can be used at home or at the practice area. They are typically designed to encourage proper physical aspects of the golf swing such as alignment, set-up, grip, or swing plane. Training aids can also include instructional video and books to teach these skills. The use of video and computer-generated devices to provide feedback to an individual's golf swing are increasingly popular as training aids.

While training aids can be very helpful in learning and improving the golf swing, they must also be well-designed and properly used. They don't need to be expensive and can often be simple items from your home or golf bag. A common example is to use two clubs to make parallel lines toward the target on the practice tee. This simple arrangement encourages proper alignment toward the target.

There are also training aids for those who want to strengthen their relationship with Christ. These include daily devotional books, Christian radio programs, inspirational music, memory verse cards, and a concordance of the Bible. But just as in golf, we need to be cautious to identify those aids that are valid and truly helpful.

SWING THOUGHT

Training aids for both our golf game and for our walk with Christ must be carefully selected and suited to our needs. Just as there are people who want to sell you a "bill of goods," so there will be ideas and ideologies that will not be an aid to your spiritual growth. That's why the Bible encourages us to be wise as serpents, but harmless as doves. The key word must always be discernment.

Live Hands; Loving Heart
Deuteronomy 6:4–9; Mark 12:28–34

KEY VERSE

You shall love the LORD your God with all your heart, and with all your soul, and with all your might. And these words which I command you this day shall be upon your heart. (Deut. 6:5–6)

E M. Prain describes the essence of his book *Live Hands* in his description of those who play with such outstanding ease, "Their hands controlled the club throughout, and they hit the ball with their hands. The class player gives an impression which I can only describe as 'live-handed.'"

He goes on to say, "His hands are always doing something. They dominate the swing to such an extent that no other movement in it stands out for all to see. It is this factor which produces a spectacle of smooth and rhythmic ease. It is this factor, too, the control for the club by the hands and the hitting of the ball with the hands through the medium of the clubhead, which makes the first-class golfer." In contrast, as week-end golfers, ". . . we are far too prone to make too much use of the body. We suffer, if you like, from too much body urge." To counter this, remember to control your swing with your hands and let your body follow.

It is "live hands" that need to control the golf swing. It is a "loving heart" that needs to control our life. The great commandment includes the admonition to *love* God with all your *heart*. It is a loving heart that is humble, open, pure, and directed toward God. It is open to God's direction and influence instead of being hardened. When a person loves God with all his heart, God is able to use and empower that person. There is an aliveness in his walk with the Lord.

SWING THOUGHT

Developing "live hands" takes practice and usually the help of a golf professional. In the same way, God will give you his own loving heart when you humble yourself in his holy presence.

$\mathcal{T}$HE GAME OF GOLF IS A GAME OF
ACCEPTING FAILURE; OF ACCEPTING
IMPERFECTION; OF REALIZING THAT
THE PERFECT GAME HAS NEVER
BEEN PLAYED, NEVER WILL BE PLAYED,
OR EVER COULD BE PLAYED.

AUTHOR UNKNOWN

Swing Thoughts for Today
Psalm 139:17–18; 23–24

KEY VERSE

Search me, O God, and know my heart! Try me and know my thoughts! (Ps. 139:23)

J ust what is a "swing thought"? Most golfers have them but do not realize there is actually a term for them. A swing thought is a mental image, word, or phrase that you visualize and/or verbalize to yourself just before and/or during your swing.

Most players have swing thoughts during a round of golf. However, most instructors agree that we should have no more than one or two swing thoughts during a round. Too many thoughts will overload you with information, making you become too mental rather than simply trusting your swing. The swing doesn't have to be complex to be efficient. Therefore, start and finish the round with just one, or possibly two, swing thoughts or images.

In this book, there are many "swing thoughts," and you have already put them to use. Just as in golf, it's helpful if you just focus on one or two of these throughout the day. The right focus can brighten your day, make you more productive and more effective, and make you a blessing to those around you.

SWING THOUGHT

This might be a good time to create two or three swing thoughts of your own.

Practice the Short Shots
Proverbs 13:11

KEY VERSE

Wealth hastily gotten will dwindle,
but he who gathers little by little will increase it. (Prov. 13:11)

 Most people don't practice enough from within sixty yards, even though 60 percent of all golf shots are within that distance. It takes discipline and commitment to practice the short game. Perhaps the difficulty of the short shots is also a reason why more people do not devote practice time to them. However, amateurs should do what the pros have learned—practice the short game.

E. M. Prain comments, "For reasons too obvious to state, of all the shots in golf the short shots are most telling. The steepest climb along the road to scratch lies between that mark and four handicap. These last few strokes are the most difficult of all to discard. As a rule, it is in the short shots that the solution lies. No one can become a good scratch golfer without an effective short game. "

He says," Rhythm in this department is essential, even more necessary perhaps than in the longer shots. Yet the same principle applies: feel the club-head and hit the ball crisply with the hands...In the short game, more than ever, we must strive to be live-handed. We can afford from the half shots downward to restrict the body turn, to stay more over the ball, and to let the hands and clubhead do the rest." We have found that there needs to be a mix of relaxed hand action with a pinch of solid forearm. You need to swing your forearms in a nice, forceful pendulum, and allow your hands to simply ride along; feel the club face, and work the blade through the ball.

It is the little things that make a difference in life as well. Seldom do we have the opportunity to make a dramatic impact. Few of us will make the limelight or be widely recognized. Certainly God is not impressed by bigness or drama. Instead we make an impact one person at a time and often in small, subtle, and unnoticed ways.

SWING THOUGHT

It's the many little things each day that occur in life that reveal the presence of God. They need practice just like the short shots in golf.

$\mathcal{T}$HE FIRST
REQUISITE
OF A TRULY
SOUND SWING
IS SIMPLICITY.

BOBBY JONES

A Good Pre-Shot Routine
Psalm 119:15

KEY VERSE

I will meditate on thy precepts, and fix my eyes on thy ways. (Ps. 119:15)

A pre-shot routine is critical before each shot. Our goal should always be to develop a consistent, predictable routine. It needs to be a brief pattern of thoughts and movements that help prepare for the execution of the swing itself.

It typically includes the following: standing a couple of paces behind the ball to focus on the line to the target; moving to the side and positioning the club face in line with the target; positioning your hands on the club (grip); and squaring your feet, shoulders, and hips to the target. Once this basic routine is part of your muscle memory, your pre-shot should be brief and natural. It boils down to "plan your shot, set up, and swing."

It is also important that we establish a "pre-shot routine" for our daily living. At first this may be a challenge to establish—just as it is in golf. But once a part of our game, it makes all the difference in the world if we are to move in the direction of our target. What is this pre-shot routine? It involves spending regular time with God, typically early in the day, by reading and meditating (thinking and reflecting) on a passage of Scripture from the Bible. You may want to use a devotional book as your guide or read through a few verses of the Bible on your own.

Your time with God each day also needs to include prayer to your heavenly Father. This prayer may take several forms: (1) adoration, (2) confession, (3) thanksgiving, and (4) supplication (asking). Or it may simply be when you talk to God about your day, asking him for help, and offering prayer for yourself and others. This is a time to talk to God. It is also a time to be still and listen to what he has to say to you. You may want to write down your requests to God, along with the answers you receive from the Father.

SWING THOUGHT

How can you modify and practice your "pre-shot" and "pre-day" routines to make them more helpful and meaningful? A good idea may be to take out a piece of paper and jot down a few things you would like from your daily time with God. Right now would be a great time to start.

Fundamentals for Golf and Life

Part Four

Grip on the Word
2 Timothy 3:14–17

KEY VERSE

All scripture is inspired by God and profitable for teaching, for reproof, for correction, and for training in righteousness, that the man of God may be complete, equipped for every good work. (2 Tim. 3:16–17)

In golf, the placement of the hands on the club is the single most important factor to influence swinging the club correctly. If the hands are not in balance, if the club is not placed in the fingers so that centrifugal force can work, if the hands do not line up with the club, and most importantly, if there is inappropriate grip pressure during the swing, it is impossible to produce accurate and powerful golf shots.

This fundamental influences the rest of the approach to the game. Without a proper handhold on the tools of golf—the clubs—a golfer will struggle to succeed in his commitment to the game and sometimes will not even know why.

The Bible is a lot like holding the club properly. It is the tool God has given us for understanding him—and for knowing what he expects from us. We often hear the phrase, "Hey, Joe, get a grip!" Not bad counsel, both in life and in golf. We must "get a grip" or a handle on God's Word to function effectively in a relationship with him and his Son, Jesus Christ. We must put his Word in our hands so we can read it and then allow its wisdom to guide our thoughts and actions. It is not to be "gripped" lightly, nor must we "strangle" it. It needs to be absorbed and applied in our life daily, and over the long haul if the rest of our "game" is going to make sense.

> ## SWING THOUGHT
>
> *Gripping the golf club properly is the key to effective golf. Gripping God's Word is the key to effective living—a life of joy and significance.*

A Live-Handed Grip
Luke 8:9–15

KEY VERSE

*And as for that in the good soil, they are those who, hearing the word, hold it fast
in an honest and good heart, and bring forth fruit with patience. (Luke 8:15)*

There are many ways to grip a golf club. While the over-lapping grip is the most popular, followed by the interlocking, there have been successful players who have used some other grip. E. M. Prain says, "Yet although they may vary in type, they all obey one principle. They grip the club in the fingers."

He goes on to add that the most important fingers in each hand are the forefinger and thumb. He says that the forefingers are like "trigger fingers" since ". . . in order to grip correctly, the forefingers are bent as if for pulling the triggers of two pistols, while the thumb rests lightly in each case against the top joint of the forefinger. In this manner the thumb and forefinger of each hand form a V on the shaft of the club. This combi-nation of forefinger and thumb is really the feeler in each hand. As they pinch against the sides of the shaft, the presence of the clubhead should become more pronounced. These two fingers in each hand are the

manipulative fingers. It is mainly through them that the clubhead is felt. They are the aids to better timing, the key to better golf."

Other keys are to grip the club lightly, and in the fingers, not the palms. A common mistake is to grip the club too tightly, especially in difficult situations. This reduces the feeling of the club and the agility of the hands and forearms.

How are we to grip God's Word? We are to take hold of it in our mind and heart and apply it to our life. We do not need to struggle to understand every detail. We are simply to understand it and apply it to our life.

SWING THOUGHT

Take hold of God's Word in your hand, hear it with your mind, and hold it fast in your heart. You do not need to understand it all. God will give you the understanding you need.

I HAVE TO RATE
A FAULTY GRIP
AS THE
MOST COMMON
CAUSE OF
BAD GOLF

TOMMY BOLT

The Live-Hands Drill
1 John 3:16; Philippians 2:1–11

KEY VERSE

*By this we know love, that he laid down his life for us; and we ought to
lay down our lives for the brethren. (1 John 3:16)*

There's a drill that most people find helpful to encourage "live hands," and to get the feeling of having the hands in control with the body, turning in response to the hands. The drill involves addressing the ball with your feet close together. Hit the ball from that position, and just let your hands and forearms guide the swing and direct the rotation of the body.

It is surprising how well you'll be able to hit any iron or wood shot from this position. It is also surprising how much feeling it can give you for a smooth, balanced swing. It will teach your body how the hands can lead the proper body turn. Prain says, "There will, of course, be a slight turning of the shoulders and hips which will come to pass in a natural manner since, by reason of the locking of the feet, there is no other means of swinging the club except by the hands and wrists."

We might add that this is a drill all golfers should use every time they're on the practice tee. Feeling the hands swing the clubhead in a circle around the body is the most important feeling any golfer can develop. The hips, the body, the legs, the shoulders—everything forms a support base for swinging the club with the hands in a circle.

It's unfortunate there is not a similar drill for developing a loving heart. It's infinitely more challenging to develop a kind and loving heart toward God and others. But Jesus did demonstrate this for us through his devotion to his Father and to us. He sacrificed his own life to do the will of the One who sent him—and that was to show his love for us. He humbled himself even unto death, the ultimate demonstration of his loving heart.

SWING THOUGHT

*If you will only ask him,
God will give you a loving heart
for himself and others.
The only drill required is
your complete trust in him.*

Steadfast Position
1 Corinthians 15:58

KEY VERSE

Be steadfast, immovable, always abounding in the work of the Lord, knowing that in the Lord your labor is not in vain. (1 Cor. 15:58)

It is a wonderful assurance to know that our labor is not in vain. Even when we cannot see the progress of our efforts, the Lord is able to use what we are doing. He sees a bigger picture and a heavenly perspective that we often do not see.

For many people what they are doing in life seems to be without purpose. Depression can result from not seeing progress and results from God's perspective. On the other hand, others are more inclined to be optimistic. They tend to see the world from a more positive perspective and are less inclined to get down on themselves and on God.

No matter what your tendency, we are to be "steadfast and immovable" in our work for the Lord. We are to know that he can use our best efforts to further the work of his kingdom. Our steadfastness and our immovable position comes from our stance with the Lord. It comes from standing firm in our conviction and in our trust of him. To rely on our own strength and view of the outcome is a self-centered perspective and reflects a lack of faith.

In golf we need a solid foundation from which to hit the ball. That steadfast and immovable position is created by the position of our feet and body at address. It is sustained by maintaining that balance through the swing. We should not swing so hard that we lose the balance or foundation. Sliding back during the backswing, or forward on the downswing, increases the risk of losing that foundation.

SWING THOUGHT

Your labor will never be in vain if you remain steadfast and immovable in your position with the Lord.

$\mathscr{A}$ GOOD
PUTTER IS
A MATCH
FOR ANYONE.
A BAD PUTTER
IS A MATCH
FOR NO ONE.

HARVEY PENICK

Alignment
Colossians 1:9–13

KEY VERSE

That you may be filled with the knowledge of his will in all spiritual wisdom and understanding, to lead a life worthy of the Lord, fully pleasing to him, bearing fruit in every good work and increasing in the knowledge of God. (Col. 1:9–10)

A lignment is positioning your body (especially your feet, hips, and shoulders) so they are in line with the target for the shot. This alignment will encourage a good swing. And, when properly aligned, that good swing will be more likely to result in a well-hit ball in the direction of the target. Admittedly, we rarely execute a perfect shot, and so the result may not be as intended. But alignment is a part of the set-up that places the body in such a position that a well-executed swing is more likely to occur and send the ball toward its target.

In our walk with Christ, *alignment* is also a key ingredient. It is an alignment of our heart, our intentions, that makes the difference. This brings us closer to being conformed to the image of our Savior and Lord, Jesus Christ. The more clearly we focus our heart on knowing and serving him, the more likely we will achieve his will for our life. Admittedly, things will go wrong and our follow-through will not always be as it should. But, if we maintain our alignment on Christ and his Word, we will be drawn back *on line*, better prepared for the goals and targets of our life.

In golf, alignment is a shot-by-shot process. When we get off alignment, we need to take the time to recheck it on the practice tee. During our time on earth we must also engage in the lifelong process of aligning and continually clarifying our focus on Christ. Obstacles come into our life and confuse us, and we drift from our intentions. Thus, we must continue to align our priorities to keep our heavenly Father at the center of our life.

SWING THOUGHT

Place an imaginary club on the ground and point it directly at Jesus Christ. As you do this, what do you feel he expects of you? In what ways do you need to adjust your alignment? What must you do to focus more intently on him? What will you need to do to stay on alignment?

Power Sources
Acts 10:34–43

KEY VERSE
God anointed Jesus of Nazareth with the Holy Spirit and with power. . . . (Acts 10:38)

There are three major sources of power in the golf swing: (1) body power, (2) arm power, and (3) wrist power. Wrist power is achieved by the proper cocking of the wrists. Most teachers suggest that the wrists should be cocked after the body and shoulders have begun to turn. The wrists must be cocked so the club shaft remains on line with the target and typically (unless you are John Daly) does not go past parallel.

If they are cocked or "loaded" in the proper manner, the wrists are said to account for 70 percent of the power in the golf swing. Certainly the body and arms are important, but it is the finesse and strength in the wrists that unleashes the power of the golf swing. This is why some relatively small golfers are able to hit the ball quite far. But those who combine these sources of power most effectively are the most powerful and accurate golfers on the course.

As human beings we also have access to many sources of power.

We have access to physical and mental power—and both of these are capable of work. Because of our mental power we have learned to harness the energy of mechanical, electrical, and atomic power, along with the power of combustible fuels. We have learned to harness the power of the wind, sun, and water.

But it is the power of the Holy Spirit that will have the most powerful and lasting impact in our lives. Receiving and releasing this power requires submission to the triune God— Father, Son, and Holy Spirit.

SWING THOUGHT

Are you fully aware of the power source that God has given you? Don't fail to understand and rely on the power of the Holy Spirit at work in your life. This would be a good day to re-evaluate your understanding of this, and begin to tap God's power as never before.

Muscle Tone
Romans 12:1–2

KEY VERSE

Do not be conformed to this world but be transformed by the renewal of your mind, that you may prove what is the will of God, what is good and acceptable and perfect. (Rom. 12:2)

It's helpful to have strength and muscle tone in the upper and lower body to hit the golf ball a great distance. This power also allows the use of more lofted clubs, making it easier to hold the green. However, this strength must be properly harnessed and trained. It can be best put into practice through proper technique.

Muscle tone is important in the hands and forearms. These are the muscles involved in a live-handed swing. In *Live Hands*, E. M. Prain puts it this way, "The more we swing the club, the more supple and sensitive the hand muscles become, and the quicker that spark is generated from the clubhead to the hands. So the first thing we must do is to tone the hand muscles." This can be done at home in an area where you can swing or even waggle the club. A weighted club stick can be helpful for developing those muscles even in the off-season or between rounds.

The good news is that we can also exercise the muscles of our spiritual life. If we think of a loving (spiritual) heart as the comparable muscle, we can exercise and make it more loving in two ways. First, we can exercise it by using it. As we learn to be increasingly sensitive to God and to those around us, we develop the ability to have a heart inclined toward God and toward those who need him. Secondly, our spiritual heart is sensitized by reading and meditating on God's Word. His Word penetrates our heart and makes us sensitive to his thoughts and desires in our life. It makes our heart more loving.

SWING THOUGHT

A club in your hand and the use of it will tone your live-handed muscles. A Bible in your hand and the application of its message of love in your life will tone your loving-heart muscles.

Unleashing Power: The Swing
Part Five

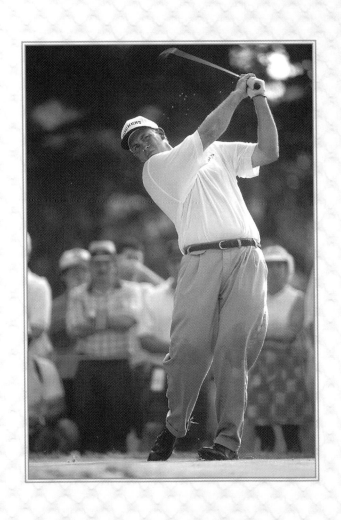

The Power of Centrifugal Force
1 Samuel 17:1–58

KEY VERSE

David put his hand in his bag and took out a stone, and slung it,
and struck the Philistine on his forehead; the stone sank into his forehead,
and he fell on his face to the ground. (1 Sam. 17:49)

You are no doubt familiar with the story of David and Goliath. It's a wonderful lesson of how God enabled a young boy to slay a giant enemy. The story teaches us to trust in God to defeat our enemies and to overcome challenges that come our way every day. It shows how God can use the most unlikely among us if we just learn to trust him and use the talents and resources he has so freely given us. It is this young lad who boldly declares to the giant, "The battle is the LORD's and he will give you into our hand."

The story of David and Goliath also illustrates a key golf principle—the power of centrifugal force. The sling and stone used by David was powerful enough to slay Goliath because of this force, along with God's power and guidance. Because of the importance of centrifugal force, we need to swing the club in a circle or arc. That circle needs to be on a plane that intersects with the location of the ball. In effect, the shoulders wind up the swing and then the arc of the clubhead goes around and through the ball. Essentially, the ball gets in the way of the clubhead as it passes through the ball on its route through the arc.

You can take a baseball swing with the club to get the feeling of this circle of centrifugal force. Gradually move the plane of that circle (and swing) toward a more vertical arc so the angle intersects with the position of the ball. It is through this circle of centrifugal force that the swing puts a ton of force behind the ball.

SWING THOUGHT

God gives us much more than the centrifugal force of a slingshot or a golf club when he works in our lives. He gives us the God-sized power of his Holy Spirit, along with the courage, power, and wisdom to slay the "giants" in our lives. Remember, the battle belongs to the Lord.

Be at Ease, Do Not Freeze
Matthew 11:28–30

KEY VERSE

For my yoke is easy, and my burden is light. (Matt. 11:30)

You can probably picture players you've seen playing golf who stood over the ball for an exceptionally long time. They seem to be frozen in a trance or perhaps caught in a routine of shifting their feet or waggling the club. For some reason, we can see this in others, but we can't seem to see it happening in ourselves.

This standing over the ball a long time occurs because many golfers think they need to ponder and ponder each shot. This is often due to a long mental checklist. They usually have no idea how long they are actually taking over each shot. Invariably the result is a poor shot.

Thinking about the shot should occur primarily before we step up to the ball. We should have a very brief, relaxed, and smooth pre-shot routine. To put it plainly, "Be at ease, do not freeze."

The impact of the pre-shot routine is important even at the very highest skill levels. For example, in the 1996 Masters, Greg Norman's pre-shot routine for the first three days lasted an average of twenty-six seconds. At the end of those three days he led the tournament by a margin of ten strokes. On the final day, when Nick Faldo overcame that lead to win the tournament, Greg's pre-shot routine averaged thirty-eight seconds. Perhaps even Greg Norman was less at ease and, therefore, thinking too much during that fourth round.

Being at ease is not all that easy. Whether in our golf swing or in the challenges of life, it is easier to suggest being at ease than to do it. We all need to simplify our lives, and enjoy the game.

SWING THOUGHT

Your long checklists for golf and life can be replaced with this simple guideline: Relax. Be at Ease!

$\mathcal{T}$HROUGH ADVERSITY
GOD REMINDS US
THAT HE WANTS US
TO GIVE HIM CONTROL
OF OUR LIFE

A Tension-Free Swing
2 Corinthians 3:17–18

—— KEY VERSE ——

Now the Lord is the Spirit, and where the Spirit of the Lord is, there is freedom. (2 Cor. 3:17)

A tension-free swing is important in any golf swing, but it is even more important on short shots than on long shots. Distance, control, and touch can only be achieved with a fluid, tension-free swing.

This is well described by E. M. Prain in the section of *Live Hands* on "Some Aids to Live-Handedness." He writes, "The short shots are best regarded simply as drives in miniature, and the same principle holds. Grip lightly; stand naturally; avoid tension; feel the clubhead in the hands; and be mindful always of its purpose, swing it with them crisply through the ball."

There are all sorts of descriptions of what this tension-free and live-handed approach might feel like. Someone once said it is like holding a tube of toothpaste just tight enough to squeeze out the amount you need, but no more. But it is more than the fingers that must reflect this lack of muscle tension. The forearms, shoulders, and legs must all be relaxed but poised.

It may be helpful to think of pitchers in baseball before they begin their windup, or a quarterback just before calling out the signals to the center and other offensive players. They are ready for action, but not tense. Too many golfers cannot say the same about their muscles just before they begin their swing. Instead they are tense and rigid.

We also need to be tension-free in our life as well as in our golf swing. Yes, it is easier said than done. And it will only come about by trusting God in our life and our swing in golf.

SWING THOUGHT

God wants to give you freedom from the worry and tension of life. All you need to do is to listen to the Instructor.

Trust Your Swing
John 14:5–14

KEY VERSE

Truly, truly, I say to you, he who believes in me will also do the works that I do; and greater works than these will he do, because I go to the Father. (John 14:12)

As a golfer you need to learn to trust your swing. Practice the golf swing on the range and learn the fundamentals. That's where you can work on corrections to the swing. There you engage in a mental checklist to help remember the key changes you are trying to make.

But on the golf course, practice time is over. Now you simply have to trust your swing. Now is when you must have confidence in your swing and not get bogged down with swing thoughts and other ideas. There is an old golfer's proverb that says, "A golfer with many swing thoughts will spend a lot of time with the squirrels."

God also wants us to trust in him. Jesus says he is the way, the truth, and the life, and that no one comes to the Father but by him. It is our privilege to entrust our life to the Lord Jesus Christ. This involves an initial release of our life to him, and then to trust him by learning to release each part of our daily life to him.

Trust is having the faith to believe that Jesus cares about you and will nurture you. It is not blind faith but a faith built on the solid foundation of the promises made in God's Word. That base is strengthened when we read his Word and practice trust and faith in daily living.

SWING THOUGHT

Trust the Lord for the "shots" you face in your life today. He promises to direct your swing.

THE GOOD PLAYER SWINGS
THROUGH THE BALL WHILE THE
AWKWARD PLAYER HITS AT IT.

KEN VENTURI

Balance
Ephesians 4:9–16

KEY VERSE

That we many no longer be children, tossed to and fro and carried about with every wind of doctrine, by the cunning of men, by their craftiness in deceitful wiles. (Eph. 4:14)

Balance typically represents something that is desirable. It is a state of equilibrium where the parts of something offset those of another. There is a balance to most everything we do in life. Even good things like exercise, eating vegetables, and drinking liquids must be done in moderation and in balance.

In the golf swing, balance is the proper distribution of the weight of the body before, during, and after the swing. This is both static and motion balance. Balance helps players achieve the full potential of their muscles—in both accuracy and distance.

Balance is something the body does naturally. Unfortunately, people do things in the golf swing that distort that natural balance. If a player learns to swing the golf club properly in a circular manner around his body, balance will take care of itself. The key is to stay in control of the swing around the body.

There is a balance in faith as well. We must be cautious not to get out on a limb of doctrine or persuasion that is extreme or contradictory to a balanced understanding of the Scripture. To become obsessed with things like the end times, gifts of the Holy Spirit, fasting, demonic influence in the world, or a particular book of the Bible have the potential of putting us out of balance. Each of these elements is a part of Scripture, but an over-emphasis on any one area is a distortion of the balanced perspective of God's Word.

SWING THOUGHT

Take the right stance, and God will give you the balance to release your full potential. He will do this today and every day of your life.

Timing
Romans 8:1–11; 1 Corinthians 2:6–16

KEY VERSE

For those who live according to the flesh set their minds on the things of the flesh, but those who live according to the Spirit set their minds on the things of the Spirit. (Rom. 8:5)

E. M. Prain teaches that "timing is the coordination of mind and muscle that brings the clubhead to the ball with the maximum speed at the moment of impact." In describing outstanding players, he says they hit the ball with the hands through the medium of the clubhead. The movements of each player's body is perfectly synchronized.

J. H. Taylor, a prominent golf instructor from the early 1900's, wrote, "The soul of golf is timing. The timing of any golf shot is felt in the motion of the clubhead, when the hands and fingers are in complete control, all through the stroke. As far as possible put your brain into your hands, let the ankles, knees and hips do their movement as subconsciously as possible, and let your thoughts live only in your hands—delicate, sensitive and obedient hands."

In order for each part of the body to be synchronized (in time with each other), some part must set the pace and be in control. That part, according to these historic teachers, is the hands. Since the hands are the only part of the body that comes in direct contact with the club, they must control the timing. They set the tempo and lead the other parts that follow.

When we invite Christ into our lives, God gives us the Holy Spirit to dwell within us. It is he who is our source of control. Like the hands that are in direct contact with the club, it is the Holy Spirit within us who gives us direct contact with the Father and with his Son, Jesus Christ.

SWING THOUGHT

Only when you allow the Holy Spirit to guide and direct your life will you have the "timing" you need to become the person God has designed you to be.

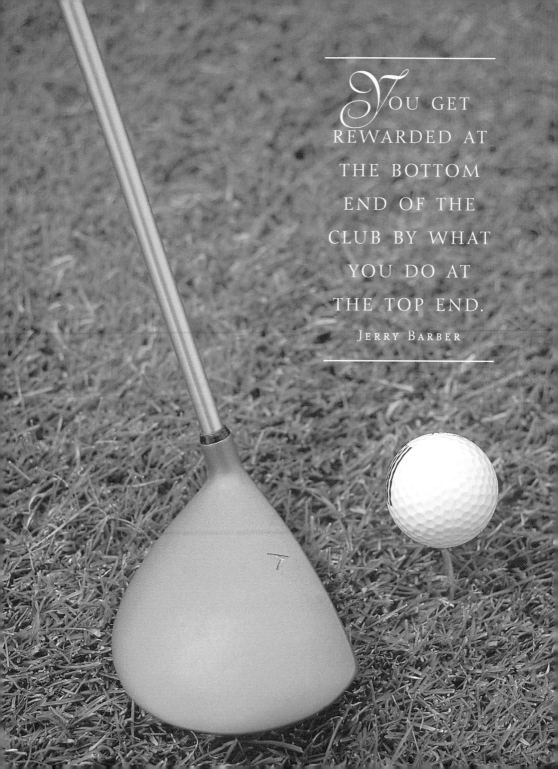

YOU GET
REWARDED AT
THE BOTTOM
END OF THE
CLUB BY WHAT
YOU DO AT
THE TOP END.

JERRY BARBER

The Release
Proverbs 3:1–12; Psalm 37:3–7

KEY VERSE

Trust in the LORD with all your heart, and do not rely on your own insight. In all your ways acknowledge him, and he will make straight your paths. (Prov. 3:5–6)

The release is one of the most subtle and difficult parts of the golf swing to grasp and to put into practice. For a gifted few it comes naturally. But for most of us it's a lifelong challenge. The secret comes in the proper release of the hands, wrists, and arms at the point of impact with the ball and in the follow-through. This release is made possible by proper coiling and cocking in the backswing.

The release is not a flip, and it is not a hinge. It is not throwing the club or clubhead at the ball. Instead, it is releasing the power of the muscles at a time that gives maximum power and accuracy. This can be felt more than it can be seen. One of the reasons, perhaps, it's such a challenge.

It's like using a broom as a club and feeling the release of the straw end of the broom as it moves through the ball position. The straw "sweeps" through the ball as the arms release the power in the forearms, wrists, and shoulder turn. The release can

also be felt with a sledge hammer when swung lightly like a club in each hand and then in both hands. The clubhead (like the hammer head) is released as it passes through the position of the ball.

Releasing our life to Christ is also a challenge for many of us to understand. We are not accustomed to "letting go and letting God!" It's not easy to learn to trust God when we are used to being in control—just as it's hard to trust our swing and release the available power at the proper time. As in golf, we have to unlearn old habits as well as acquire new ones. The secret is faith and trust.

SWING THOUGHT

The full, natural release of your life to God, like the release of your swing in golf, can only be achieved by letting go, and allowing yourself to feel (experience) the freedom and power so readily available. The power is there. It just needs to be recognized and tapped.

The Gallery Finish
1 Thessalonians 2:2–8

KEY VERSE

So we speak, not to please men, but to please God who tests our hearts. (1 Thess. 2:4)

The proper completion of the golf swing has been referred to as the "gallery finish." It is at the very extension of the swing when the clubhead and arms have reached the end of their arc. At this point, if done properly, the whole weight of the body has flowed in behind the shot. The hands are high and fully in front of and around the body. The club shaft is now nearly parallel to the shoulders and behind them. The body remains in balance despite having hit the ball with a full ton of pressure. Without supple muscles it is not even possible to get to such a position.

The great golfers tend to hold this position for a moment as they complete the swing. It is that pose at the end of the swing that is called a "gallery" finish because it looks so good to the gallery viewing the shot—and in photos of the finish of the swing.

If the golfer were simply trying to impress the gallery, he would be wasting his time. In fact, it would be a rather vain practice. However, this beautiful finish is usually the result of some excellent swing skills that are effective in ball striking. It is only because of the effectiveness of those swing skills that anyone should care to have a "gallery" finish.

So it is with Paul in his letter to the Thessalonians. Paul was speaking not to please men, but to please God. He knew it was important to follow the leading of God rather than be influenced by what people might expect, want, or praise him for doing.

SWING THOUGHT

Throughout today, focus on God's expectations for you, not on the flattery and high hopes of people in the gallery of your life.

Facing Adversity
Part Six

Adversity Is God's Opportunity
Matthew 14:22–28

KEY VERSE

He spoke to them, saying, "Take heart, it is I; have no fear." (Matt. 14:27)

Some have said that adversity is just another name for the game of golf. It would be a boring experience if the golf course did not include those elements that create adversity, such as sand traps, rough, bunkers, water, dog legs, trees, shape and slope of greens, and fairways. We know what's up ahead. The challenge is to remember it and to practice for the adversity we know we will encounter.

While *anticipation* helps to avoid adversity on the golf course, *practice* will improve your ability to recover from the adversity. Certain types of adversity may be especially troubling for you. It is wise to focus on learning both to avoid and recover from those particular types of adversity.

Isn't it the same way in life? We know there will be adversity in our life. In fact, we can count on it just about every day. And some days it will be more troubling than others.

A biblical example of adversity is found in Matthew 14:22–33. After feeding the five thousand, Jesus sent the disciples to the other side of the Sea of Galilee—directly into a major storm, definitely a moment of adversity. The water and high winds seemed overwhelming. But it was also God's opportunity to remind the disciples that he was in control of the elements. Would you agree that God continues to use adversity today? When he does, it helps us remember that he is in charge of what happens in our life and in the world around us.

SWING THOUGHT

If you are facing adversity today, ask Jesus Christ to come and calm the waves and the winds of your troubles. He promises to stick closer to you than a brother. Take him up on his generous promise.

71

Focus on the Target, Not the Adversity
Matthew 14:28–33

KEY VERSE

When he saw the wind, he was afraid, and beginning to sink he cried out, "Lord, save me." (Matt. 14:30)

After Jesus walks on the water to the boat, the level of adversity increases for Peter. When Peter sees Jesus approaching, he asks the Master to invite him to walk on the water toward him. Perhaps this indicates Peter had already learned to wait for direction before stepping out on his own.

But what happens to Peter as he begins to walk on the water toward Jesus? He "saw the wind," and if he did not look down and also see the water, he had a stronger faith than most of us. We are too often tempted to look at the adversity, "the wind and the water," and to be overwhelmed by them. They seem insurmountable by our strength alone. We often see no way to face the challenges of nature, people, money, or other circumstances that threaten to pull us under.

Unlike Peter, we may even forget to seek God's direction in the first place. Therefore, we step out before knowing what Jesus wants us to do or where he wants us to go. And, like Peter, we often lose sight of the One who is able to save us from these circumstances. We take our eyes off of the One who has bid us to come to him "on the water" of our circumstances.

In golf it is easy to become too focused on the surrounding adversity. It is far better to concentrate on the target. When we focus our thoughts and eyesight on the objective of our next shot, we are more likely to avoid the adversity.

SWING THOUGHT

Today, pay special attention to keeping your eyes and mind focused on Jesus. Your loving heavenly Father promises to give you his guidance and direction.

To CONTROL YOUR NERVES,
YOU MUST HAVE A POSITIVE
THOUGHT IN YOUR MIND.

Byron Nelson

WHEN YOU MISS A SHOT,
NEVER THINK OF WHAT
YOU DID WRONG.
COME UP TO THE NEXT SHOT
THINKING OF WHAT YOU
MUST DO RIGHT.

TOMMY ARMOUR

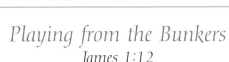

Playing from the Bunkers
James 1:12

KEY VERSE

Blessed is the man who endures trials, for when he has stood the test he will receive the crown of life which God has promised to those who love him. (James 1:12)

Many people dislike playing from the bunkers, especially fairway bunkers. First, it's a nasty reminder that the prior shot was a poor one. Second, it's hard to play from fairway bunkers. It is difficult to hit the ball cleanly and to judge how far it will go. While pros make it look easy, it is a grueling challenge for most amateurs.

Facing the challenge of a difficult bunker shot can be a reminder of just how comfortable it is to play from the fairway. Occasionally, we all need that reminder. Learning to play from bunkers can also help us learn to play better from the preferred lie in the fairway.

Life teaches us a similar lesson. The "bunkers" of our daily existence are inevitable. We might as well accept the fact that hardships are going to come to us, to members of our family, and our friends.

Even before finding ourselves in one of life's "bunkers," it's best to learn the keys to getting back out. It doesn't help to complain and moan. Instead, we must assess the situation, ask for some counsel, pray to God for help, and then take our best shot. If you are still "in the bunker" or have landed in another one, don't give up. Learn from your first attempt and then try again.

SWING THOUGHT

So you're in one of life's "bunkers" today? You hit it in there; now hit it out!

Play It as It Lies
Jeremiah 17:5–8

KEY VERSE

Blessed is the man who trusts in the LORD, whose trust is in the LORD.
He is like a tree planted by water, that sends out its roots by the stream. . . . (Jer. 17:7–8)

Too many amateur golfers are inclined to play "winter rules," even during the perfect conditions of summer. They move the ball into their own fairway, perhaps even in the rough, before hitting it.

The more serious golfer will typically play it as it lies. There are many advantages to doing this. One is that it gives you practice hitting the ball from the kinds of lies that occur on the golf course—a ball sitting in a deep divot, nasty sloping lies, and those bothersome tufts of grass behind the ball. Then, in tournament play, the player is more prepared for those uncomfortable situations. Furthermore, for the purist, it's simply a matter of playing each round according to the rules so you have the satisfaction of knowing your true score.

The habit of playing properly also helps when playing in competition and tournaments. You wouldn't want to mistakenly bump the ball or commit some other unsavory infraction such as taking a gimme or tapping in quickly and accidentally missing the putt.

In life we also must "play it as it lies." There are no free lifts or "bumps." We have to learn to deal with the circumstances that come our way. Difficult situations are simply a part of life. Maturity comes as we learn to cope with these challenges and allow them to make us stronger people.

SWING THOUGHT

Trust God to give you the ability (provision) to play out of any difficult "lie" that comes your way. He will hear your prayer and give you the courage you need to play on.

Discipline to Endure
Hebrews 12:3–11

KEY VERSE

The Lord disciplines him whom he loves,
and chastises every son whom he receives. (Heb. 12:6)

In Hebrews 12:2–3 we are reminded of the hostility Jesus endured so that we need not grow weary or fainthearted. Then, in verse six, we learn that the Lord disciplines those He loves. God treats us as sons and daughters and will never fail to discipline us for our good. This is how we are trained for holiness—by the discipline of God.

The remarkable thing is that through his love he disciplines us so that we can share in his holiness. It is training in God's school that produces Christian maturity.

The hazards of the golf course are much like this. The rough, OB stakes, fairway and greenside bunkers, and water hazards are forms of discipline put there by the designer of the golf course. The designer placed those hazards in locations he knew would discipline you as a golfer. The unique location of each hazard forces you to play your best and to become a better golfer.

Over time you should become better at avoiding those hazards and getting out of them. As you get better at this, your score will improve and your appreciation for the purpose of those challenges will increase.

Are there hazards to endure in your life today? Were they placed there by God, by other people, or have you created them yourself? Whatever your answer, you can use those hazards as a source of learning and strengthening. See them as opportunities to improve and become better prepared for future obstacles that will come your way. If they are from God, remember that he has put them there out of love for you as his child.

SWING THOUGHT

Discipline, like the hazards of the course, is placed strategically in our path as a reflection of God's desire for us to grow in his wisdom and love.

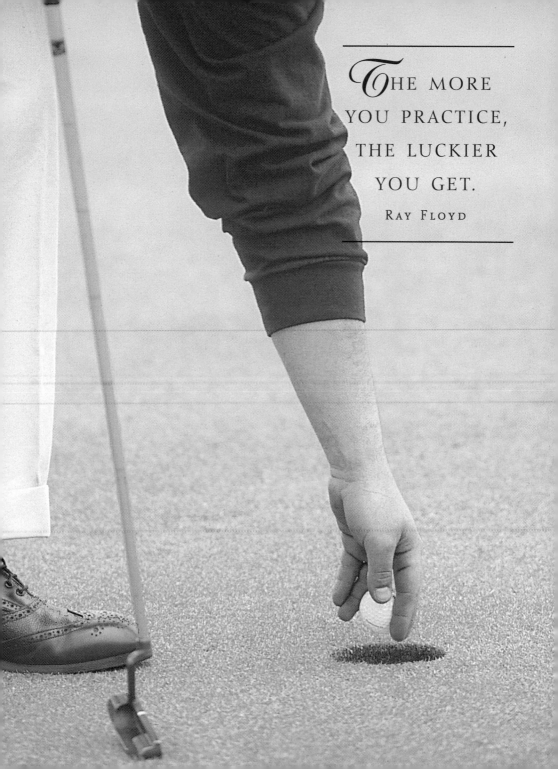

THE MORE
YOU PRACTICE,
THE LUCKIER
YOU GET.

RAY FLOYD

Prayer and Praise to God
to *God*
Part Seven

The Course Designer
Revelation 4:11

KEY VERSE

*Worthy art thou, our Lord and God, to receive glory and honor and power,
for thou didst create all things, and by thy will they existed and were created.* (Rev. 4:11)

It is often revealing to know who designed a golf course. Certain designers are known for the unique styles and features they put into their courses. It may be their use of certain types of traps, the building materials they prefer for retaining walls, or the size and elevation of their greens. Some are known to be great course designers because of their own ability or the skills of a team of people assembled to design and build quality courses.

The ultimate designer of the golf course on which we play every day of our lives is, of course, God himself. He is the author and the creator of the universe. He has created and displayed nature as we know it. Any human golf course designer can only work within the boundaries of what God has created.

It is only when course designers use their imagination and ingenuity to make the best use of God's creation that truly exceptional golf courses are created. In those situations a beautiful piece of nature is transformed into a place where people who love to play golf are challenged to try their skills. The result is a symphony of golfing ability played in concert with the challenges and pleasures of the beauty of nature that surrounds the eighteen holes.

That symphony is made more beautiful by the realization that God has created all things—including us. For this reason, the beauty and the praise for his creation must ultimately be given to him.

SWING THOUGHT

Message to the greatest Designer of all: "Worthy art thou, our Lord and God, to receive glory and honor and power."

Alignment of Head and Eyes
Hebrews 12:1–11

KEY VERSE

Looking to Jesus the pioneer and perfecter of our faith. . . . (Heb. 12:2)

Brian Mogg, former tour professional, uses an interesting tool to help align the head and eyes for putting. It has a significant application to our lives as well.

Brian suggests placing a small mirror directly behind the ball and then aligning the putter in the normal manner. If your head is properly positioned over and just behind the ball, you will see your eyes reflected back at you in the mirror.

If you do not see the reflection of your eyes in the mirror, adjust your position until you are comfortable in your stance and able to see your eyes in the mirror. Putting from that position should help the putt feel solid and be on line. It helps to give you the alignment needed for a solid and straight putt.

Proper alignment in life comes when we focus our eyes directly into the eyes of Christ. He will reflect the true picture of who we are, how much we need him, and his great desire to give direction to our life. We are to position ourselves and align our actions to be consistent with his expectations.

When we get out of alignment with Christ we need to adjust our stance and perspective. God's Word, the guidance of the Holy Spirit, and the encouragement of friends in Christ are key sources to help keep us moving in the right direction.

SWING THOUGHT

Jesus wants you to position yourself so that he can reflect his love, grace, and direction for your life. All it takes is a "mirror" in which you will be able to see his face.

GIVEN AN EQUALITY OF STRENGTH
AND SKILL, THE VICTORY IN GOLF
WILL BE TO HIM WHO IS
CAPTAIN OF HIS SOUL.

ARNOLD HAULTAIN

Constant in Prayer
Romans 12:12

KEY VERSE

Rejoice in your hope, be patient in tribulation, be constant in prayer. (Rom. 12:12)

Have you ever wondered what it would be like to begin the final day of a major championship with a slight lead or even with a realistic shot at winning the tournament? What would you think about and try to do?

Romans 12:12 seems uniquely suited to such a situation. It seems you would want to begin the day's round "rejoicing in hope." But big tournament or not, you need to start each day, and each round of life, rejoicing in the hope and opportunity that God has given you.

Next you would want to find the grace to "be patient in tribulation."

There's no question about it: you *will* face tribulation in a round of golf. Golf is designed that way, and major tournaments are designed for tribulation. And so is life. Not every day will have you crawling up the wall, but you need to realize that trials and tribulation will come sooner or later.

Finally, you would want to be "constant in prayer." You cannot be praying every moment of the round (or day), but you can pray before the round. And during the round you can devote your game and skills to serve the Lord. That is the way you should begin and live each day. There should be constant prayer in your heart.

Unlike a major golf championship, your daily drama is probably not as intense, nor is it publicly recorded by television cameras and the print media. Still, you need to live each day by the key points in this verse.

SWING THOUGHT

When your life looks and feels like the challenge of the final round of a major golf championship, face it with rejoicing, patience, and prayer. God promises that, in the end, you will be a winner.

Playing Amen Corner
1 Thessalonians 5:17; 3:10; Ephesians 6:18

KEY VERSE
Pray constantly. . . . (1 Thess. 5:17)

Have you ever thought about the name given to the area of Augusta National called "Amen Corner"? The challenge and pitfalls of holes eleven through thirteen on the back nine of the Masters is enough to bring an amen to the lips of those who manage to make it through them without disaster.

Frankly, too seldom do we pause to say "Amen" or "Thank you Lord" after traveling through difficult territory in our lives. It would probably even be better to pray *before* starting to play those holes, rather than offering a simple amen after completing them.

Do you wait until you are out of trouble to call upon God? Not only should we be in prayer in advance of all situations, but we should also pray constantly, without ever stopping. While we cannot literally have a prayer on our lips at all times, we can seek the Lord in all things and at all times. We can practice the presence of God and approach life with an attitude of prayer and thanksgiving.

We should approach our "amen corners" in prayer and seek God's grace, power, and love to see us through. This means praying in advance for the difficult decisions and challenging circumstances any given day may hold for us. It also means we need to be in touch with God during these trying situations. Finally, it means thanking him afterward—like saying "amen" and meaning it.

SWING THOUGHT

Pray constantly that God will be with you and direct your path as you go through the "amen corners" in the course of your life. This attitude of praise can— and will—change your life.

Dealing with the Sin in Your Life
Part Eight

The Core Is in Character
Hebrews 4:13

KEY VERSE

*And before him no creature is hidden, but all are open and laid bare
to the eyes of him with whom we have to do.* (Heb. 4:13)

"In football and hockey you come to intimate and often forcible contact with the outer man. Chess is a clash of intellect. But in golf, character is laid bare to character." (Arnold Haultain in *Live Hands*)

Character. The core of golf. It takes character to "step up and hit it" when there's a lake to cut across, and you're one stroke behind in the club championship. It takes character not to touch the ball slightly to move it from an old divot; it takes character to count a stroke on yourself when the ball moves slightly on the green as you address it; or to go back to the tee when your drive is about an inch out of bounds on an imaginary line between two white stakes.

Character is also at the core of life. After winning the 1996 PGA Championship, Mark Brooks said, "I have learned long ago that who I am is not what I shot today." In life, character has little to do with what we earn, whom we beat out for the promotion, the people we know,

what we wear, or where we wear it. It boils down to character in the form of who we are when stripped naked and standing before God. God already knows our true character, and he is more interested in our potential than in revealing the flaws of our past.

SWING THOUGHT

When laid bare to the issue of character, where do you stand today? Are you willing to be straight with God about that, and then be honest with yourself and two or three others? Accountability to God and to those you trust is a great character booster.

The "S" Word
Romans 7:13–25; 6:23

KEY VERSE

I do not understand my own actions. For I do not do what I want,
but I do the very thing I hate. (Rom. 7:15)

 t times it seems as if Paul might actually have been a golfer. In this key verse it sounds like he is describing the unspeakable shank. Anyone who has experienced this dreadful malady senses that Paul is writing out of his own experience with the shanks or perhaps the dreaded yips in putting.

Actually, Paul is writing about what he has experienced firsthand: sinning. He is saying, with sorrow and regret, that he does the very thing he hates. As much as he may try to be without sin, he recognizes that he continues to put distance between himself and God. He says in verse eighteen, "For I do not do the good I want, but the evil I do not want is what I do."

We must all come to the point of recognizing that we do sin and we will sin. While it causes us sorrow and concern, we must also recognize that Christ has already chosen to pay the penalty for our sin. This is the good news that is repeated several places throughout the New Testament.

The first three verses of the eighth chapter of Romans is a good example: *There is therefore now no condemnation for those who are in Christ Jesus. For the law of the Spirit of life in Christ Jesus has set me free from the law of sin and death. For God has done what the law, weakened by the flesh, could not do; sending his own Son in the likeness of sinful flesh and for sin, he condemned sin in the flesh.*

SWING THOUGHT

Jesus wants to forgive you and give you peace this day and for eternity. Yes, you will shank the ball both on and off the course. But your Instructor is close by. Your only obligation is to pay attention to— and do—what he has to tell you.

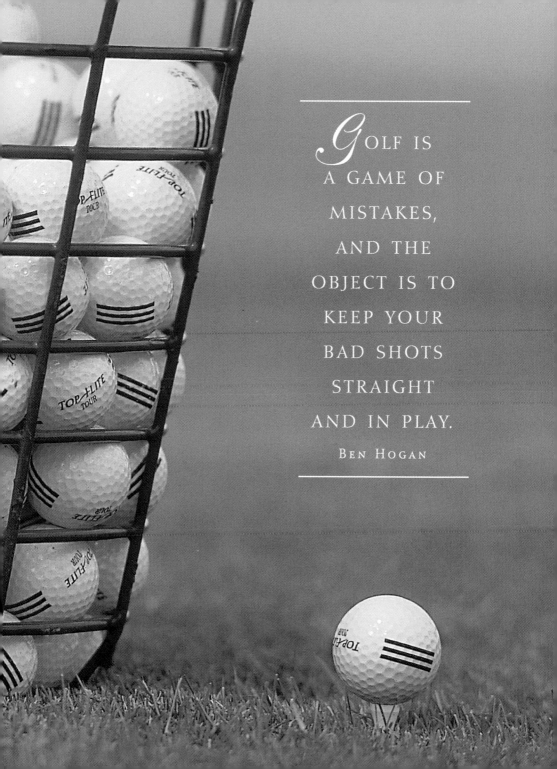

GOLF IS
A GAME OF
MISTAKES,
AND THE
OBJECT IS TO
KEEP YOUR
BAD SHOTS
STRAIGHT
AND IN PLAY.
BEN HOGAN

Sin of Pride
Proverbs 8:13; 11:2; 16:18

KEY VERSE

Pride goes before destruction, and a haughty spirit before a fall. (Prov. 16:18)

P ride is the root of all sin. It is the mistaken notion that we are in control instead of allowing God to be the master of our lives. This is what makes pride the ultimate sin—alienation that will always keep us from being dependent on God.

The three passages in Proverbs are just a few of the many places in the Bible where God gives us insight about this area of sin in our life. In these passages we learn that:

-God hates pride and arrogance

-Pride leads to disgrace, but humility leads to wisdom

-Pride and a haughty spirit go before destruction

It is patently clear that God is not pleased with pride in our lives. When we are self-centered and choose a life of self-reliance, we go against God's commands and his desire for our life. He wants us to be confident and bold, but reliant on him. Clearly, pride leads to negative consequences for us . . . including disgrace and destruction.

Golf provides an excellent illustration of this. Unfortunately, a par (for high handicappers), a birdie (for lower handicappers), or a string of birdies (for professionals) is too often followed by a bad shot or a bad hole. After good fortune we tend to forget the key thoughts and concentration that got us there. It is as though we allow pride to enter into our thinking and distract us.

SWING THOUGHT

Are you relying on yourself or on God to help you in the key areas of your life? It's a question to ask yourself today—and every day.

Confession of Sin
1 John 1:5–10

KEY VERSE

*If we confess our sins, he is faithful and just and will
forgive us our sins and purify us from all unrighteousness.* (1 John 1:9)

To achieve proper clubhead speed and direction in the golf swing, it is vital to turn fully and coil your back and shoulder muscles in the backswing. They need to be fully "loaded" to be in position to make the correct downswing move. Without this correct coiling position, it is virtually impossible to be in the right position to hit the ball on the downswing.

Just as in the golf swing, where we need to coil in the backswing to be in position to hit the ball, so spiritually we must make a move to get us into the correct relationship with God. (Actually, he has already made the first move of showing his love to us through the life, death, and resurrection of his Son Jesus Christ.)

Our initial move is to acknowledge our sinfulness before him, and declare our inability to save ourselves. This is the key step needed to be in position where we can enjoy a correct relationship (or proper position) with God. Sin will separate us from God until we get to this position with him.

Once we confess our sins and acknowledge that he is Lord of our life, then he will forgive our sins and cleanse us from all unrighteousness.

> ## SWING THOUGHT
>
> *Confession of sin is a prayer that puts you in a right position spiritually with God. Is there something you feel you need to share with God now? He is the best listening friend you will ever have.*

*A*LL GOLF IS DIVIDED
INTO THREE PARTS...
THE STROKES, THE COURSE,
AND THE OPPONENT.

TOMMY ARMOUR

Life's Biggest "Gimme"
Romans 3:21–26; 5:18–21; 6:23

KEY VERSE

For the wages of sin is death, but the free gift of God
is eternal life in Christ Jesus our Lord. (Rom. 6:23)

Golfers know that a "gimme" is a term used to tell a player that the other players are "giving" him the putt. The player can pick up his ball and count one stroke (the remaining putt) as his final stroke on the hole. The expression to the player is "That's a gimme."

The player given this "gift" is to pick up the ball. If the choice is *not* to accept the gimme and go ahead and putt the ball, the player is on his own. If the player doesn't make the putt, he has to count his score including whatever number of putts it takes to get in the hole. In other words, if the player does not accept the "gimme," he has to finish the hole and take the consequences for the score.

But there's another, bigger "gimme" in life. It's the gift of eternal life offered by Jesus Christ through his death on the cross—a gift that tells the world Jesus gave his life as payment for our sins. All we need to do is accept this gift. The consequence of not accepting is that we are left to our own devices— hoping against hope that we can somehow *make it*. There is no way we can earn God's favor on our own merits. No one is good enough on his own, because we have all sinned and we fall short of God's expectations.

If we choose not to take the gimme God has given us, we will then spend eternity without God. The name for that place is hell—a terrible and eternal separation from God.

SWING THOUGHT

God is offering you the greatest gimme of your life. Will you say "yes" to his generous offer and let him bear the burden of your sin? To say "yes" is a lot like getting a gimme from the tee box on a long par five . . . unbelievable, but true.

Christ Is the Answer
Part Nine

Recruiting for God's Squad
John 3:11–21

KEY VERSE

Truly, truly, I say to you, we speak of what we know, and bear witness to what we have seen; but you did not receive our testimony. (John 3:11)

A large part of the vision of the LINKS Players Association is that golfers will recognize that golf offers an opportunity to share Christ with others. Those who love God will want to consider how they can use their involvement in golf as a witness to those who participate in the game with them.

Jim Hiskey of the LINKS Players Association says, "It's like recruiting. My coach did it at the University of Houston. He wanted a team that could win the NCAA championship. He called me in Idaho one day and invited me to join his team. And because he was a good recruiter I had the pleasure to play on his first three NCAA championship teams."

God wants us to be recruiters of followers of Jesus Christ. That is what the Great Commission is all about. It just so happens that the game of golf has some similar characteristics. These similarities give us the opportunity to meet and encourage people who, like each of us, need to get to know the greatest coach there is—or ever was—the person of Jesus Christ.

We need to be recruiters and to encourage those we recruit to be recruiters. Paul did this with Timothy, and Timothy did it with others. It's a multiplication process that began 2000 years ago, and one that's taking hold in the realm of golf throughout the world.

SWING THOUGHT

What is there about your life that would attract people to play with you on God's team? List two or three things you feel best describe where you are in your walk with Christ.

Golf—A Metaphor for Life
Romans 6:23; 8:1–11

KEY VERSE

For the wages of sin is death, but the free gift of God is eternal life in Christ Jesus our Lord.
(Rom. 6:23)

Larry Moody, chaplain to the PGA tour players and president of Search Ministries, has described golf as a marvelous metaphor for life. He points out that we are never good enough at golf to satisfy our desire for perfection. There are always strokes we know we could have eliminated. Even in record-setting rounds in the major championships, the players look back and see where they could have cut some strokes.

So it is in life. None of us are so good that we can get to heaven on our own merits. Paul tells us we have all have fallen short of the test of being without sin. No one is able to live this life and be error free. Only Christ was able to accomplish that. However, none of us are so bad that we will not be able to spend eternity with our heavenly Father. That's because Jesus has paid the price for all our sins, regardless of their severity or frequency.

At the 1996 World Links Conference at Callaway Gardens in Georgia, Larry described how the letters in the word *golf* can summarize the options available to each of us. The first option is to leave this earth without knowing Jesus Christ as personal Lord and Savior. On the other hand, the word *golf* can be used to summarize the promises available to every individual on earth.

G oing		G od
O ut	–or–	O ffers
L ost		L ove and
F orever		F orgiveness

SWING THOUGHT

GOLF will either spell DISASTER or GLORY. The eternal choice is yours.

The Master's Ticket
Revelation 3:20; John 14:1–7

KEY VERSE

*Behold, I stand at the door and knock. If anyone hears my voice and opens the door,
I will come in and eat with him, and he with me. (Rev. 3:20)*

Each year there are people outside the entrance to the Master's Championship who are wearing or carrying signs reading, I NEED A TICKET. It is ironic that people recognize and advertise their need for a ticket to a wonderful athletic event but do not recognize their need for a ticket to spend eternity with God.

People want a ticket to the Master's golf tournament for the sheer beauty of the place, the courtesy and tradition that surround the event, the opportunity to see the incredible talent of the players, and to experience the drama that surrounds virtually every shot.

A one-way ticket to heaven certainly ought to be even more valued and sought after than a ticket to a golf event. If these ticket-seekers knew what they were missing, they would carry a sign asking for a different kind of ticket, one that might read: I NEED THE TICKET TO HEAVEN.

This true Master's ticket is, amazingly, a free one. It cannot be earned, purchased, or stolen from its rightful owner. The price of the ticket has already been paid by Christ through his death on the cross, through the miracle of his resurrection from the dead.

But, like the Master's tournament, not everyone who shows up at the gate gets to enter. The true Master's ticket to heaven is actually easier to get than the one in Georgia. This ticket to heaven is acquired by a simple act of obedience to Jesus' command to come to the Father through him. It requires accepting that Jesus died for your sins and, that you are, therefore, forgiven by God.

SWING THOUGHT

When you carry a sign saying, I NEED A TICKET, make sure you are asking for the ticket that will do you the most good—the only ticket, in fact, that will ultimately matter.

A Game of Opposites
Luke 9:23–25

KEY VERSE

*For whoever would save his life will lose it; and whoever
loses his life for my sake, he will save it.* (Luke 9:24)

The game of golf is a game of opposites. Examples are numerous. Bobby Jones pointed out that "to cure a slice you have to learn to aim where you don't want the ball to go." The natural tendency for the "slicer" is to aim further and further left, the effect of which is to emphasize the slice even more. Instead, if golfers will practice aiming to the right, they will begin to learn how to "get through the ball" so they no longer maintain the tendency to stop at the ball or cut across it, action that creates the slice.

Another of golf's opposites is that when we most need to relax our arms and shoulders to hit a difficult shot, we are usually most inclined to tighten our muscles. The result is that we tend to make our worst shot when we most need a good shot . . . like over a water hazard. We know golf is a game of opposites because we always seem to be so surprised to find that the easier we swing, the farther the ball carries. We know it is

true, but we keep wanting to swing hard, grunt loudly, and somehow power the ball with brute strength. We resist the idea of doing the opposite of what seems natural.

Sometimes things in life are also opposite of what our human minds would think. Several examples are found in Scripture and in our relationship with Jesus. For example, Jesus said that he who is to gain his life must first lose it. Even his own life was opposite to what most people expected. People expected a Messiah who would come to destroy those who ruled over them here on earth. Instead, Jesus came and gave his life for others so that his Kingdom would be eternal.

SWING THOUGHT

*The more we give up to God
the more he gives to us. What
"opposite" thinking is God asking
you to consider today?*

YOU MUST HAVE CONFIDENCE
IN YOUR ABILITY TO MAKE
THE SHOT REQUIRED.
THIS COMES FROM PRACTICE.

BYRON NELSON

GOLF IS THE ONLY SPORT WHERE THERE ARE MORE TEACHERS THAN PLAYERS.

CONRAD REHLING

God's Spirit at Work in Us
Part Ten

Servants of Christ
2 Corinthians 11:23–29

KEY VERSE

. . . in toil and hardship, through many a sleepless night, in hunger and thirst, often without food, in cold and exposure. (2 Cor. 11:27)

Paul was what you would call a model servant of Jesus Christ. In these passages, he defends himself, and describes what he has endured for the cause of Christ, differentiating himself from those who claim to be righteous and worthy. He explains why he is a better servant of Christ than his antagonists. He describes his labors, imprisonment, beatings—often tortured to near death—along with the dangers of travel.

In golf we also have a model of servanthood. The tour caddie often endures sleepless nights, hunger and thirst, and, at times, cold and extreme exposure. But the key to the caddie's model of servanthood is in how he helps the pro perform well without getting in the way. The caddie's job is to find ways to help the pro succeed and avoid distraction.

While caddies are servants, they are also partners. They walk side-by-side with the pro, look over the shoulder, and stay behind to replace a divot or rake a bunker. This is done quietly and without recognition.

Christ, too, wants us to be his servants, while at the same time being a joint heir to his kingdom. As we serve him, we grow and share in the fruits of his realm. This means we will encounter the challenges of difficult places, rough times, terrain, and weather.

SWING THOUGHT

Are you a good servant of Jesus Christ? Do you find yourself willing to submit yourself to his regimen? Do you refuse to take the credit so that he can receive the glory in your life?

The Fruit of Your Labor
Galatians 5:22–24

KEY VERSE

But the fruit of the Spirit is love, joy, peace, patience, kindness, goodness, faithfulness, gentleness, self-control; against such there is no law. (Gal. 5:22–23)

The fruit of something is defined by Webster's dictionary as "the result, product, or consequence of any action." What is the "fruit" of your golf? Not the fruit of any one round, but the fruit over time?

For most people the fruit of golf is lasting friendships, the benefits of exercise, the satisfaction of improved skills, and an appreciation for the beauty of nature. For some, there may also be negative consequences such as lost friends, wasted time, poorly spent or lost money, and time that could have been better spent with family or at work.

If we invest ourselves in our golf game in the right way and with the right attitudes, there's little question that we will enjoy the positive fruits of the game. It will be a blessing to us, and we will be a blessing to those around us.

This passage in Galatians suggests that the fruit of the Holy Spirit at work within an individual, over time, will be an increased level and quality of love, joy, peace, patience, kindness, goodness, faithfulness, gentleness, and self-control.

With the help of the Holy Spirit, this fruit is demonstrated in our life as we allow our heavenly Father to work in us. It is not so much what we do but rather what we let the Spirit do in and through us.

SWING THOUGHT

When we allow the Spirit of God to change us and put us to useful service, we will begin to see the fruit of our labor.

It's in the Bag
Ephesians 6:10–20

KEY VERSE

Finally, be strong in the Lord and in the strength of his might. Put on the whole armor of God, that you may be able to stand against the wiles of the devil. (Eph. 6:10–11)

Frank Catania is the subject of a book entitled *Eat, Drink, and Be Merry . . . for Tomorrow We Die.* It tells of his life of crime and imprisonment before coming to know Christ. Since his repentance, he has served as an evangelist and gospel singer in a prison ministry. Frank has also become an avid golfer and enjoys sharing a spiritual lesson that was illustrated for him on the golf course.

On the number one hole at a course he played regularly, he often found himself hooking the ball left into a grove of trees. On one occasion he was prepared to use a low lofted iron to punch out of those trees as he normally did from that location. His fellow golfers questioned what he was doing. He explained that this happened a lot and he had learned to punch out to the safety of the fairway.

Hearing this they asked if he had a seven wood. They explained that he could use the seven wood to hit out and over the tops of the trees in the direction of the green. He was successful on his first try and subsequently used a seven wood routinely from that location.

He also recognized a spiritual application. God has given us spiritual armor to use for the battle we face. That armor is both offensive and defensive gear for the battle against the principalities, powers, world rulers of this present darkness, and spiritual hosts of wickedness in the heavenly places. Unfortunately, many individuals do not know how to use, or remember to use this armor.

SWING THOUGHT

Do you know how and when to use the spiritual armor of truth, righteousness, peace, faith, salvation, and the Spirit? It's in your bag! Learn to use it when needed and appropriate.

No Timidity Allowed
2 Timothy 1:7

KEY VERSE

God did not give us a spirit of timidity but a
spirit of power and love and self-control. (2 Tim. 1:7)

In golf, being too timid is usually a mistake, just as being too intense can also lead to difficulties. Examples of timidity turned sour are those times when tour professionals have lowered their intensity once they were in a commanding lead, only to let their game slip away from them and lose the tournament.

Another example is where a player becomes too tentative on a chip or pitch shot only to fall well short of the green or pin. It is the result of being too tentative and not following through on the shot. While being overly aggressive is also a problem, being too tentative or timid is a common problem.

But, what does the verse mean in a spiritual sense? It should serve as a reminder that the believer in Christ has been given the gift of the Holy Spirit. Christians are therefore reminded they are not to be timid in their walk of faith. Instead, they are to use the power, love, and self-control that is theirs through the work of the Spirit in their life.

Only you and God know where he wants you to be less timid today and in the days ahead. Only you and God know where it is that the Spirit can help you to exhibit God's power, love, and self-control. Don't be shy about asking for his wisdom. He promises to offer it freely.

SWING THOUGHT

With God's power, love, and self-control at work in your life, you will no longer need to be timid. You can even be bold in pursuing the things that are beyond your own natural capability.

106

THE PERSON I FEAR MOST IN THE
LAST TWO ROUNDS IS MYSELF.

TOM WATSON

Playing with Patience
Colossians 3:12; James 5:7-11

KEY VERSE

Put on then, as God's chosen ones, holy and beloved, compassion,
kindness, lowliness, meekness, and patience. (Col. 3:12)

In *Golf Illustrated* Bobby Clampett stated, "No game has ever required the character trait of patience more than the game of golf. A patient attitude is a never-give-up attitude. Without patience you cannot be a consistent performer; without patience you cannot reach your potential; without patience you cannot win."

He describes his own "destruction" in the 1982 British Open as he fell to a tenth-place tie after a seven stroke lead during the third round. Bobby says that he and his playing partner Nick Price had ". . . both been guilty of being impatient and impulsive,

externalizing the anxiety that mounted from the pressure of winning."

Bobby points out that every culture sees patience as a prerequisite for success. He writes: "The Japanese say, 'In whatever you do, unless you have patience you will not succeed.' The Irish put it this way: 'Patience is a plaster for every wound.' In England, it's 'Beware the fury of a patient man.' Benjamin Franklin once advised, 'He that can have patience can have what he will.'"

Why is such a clearly recognized and sorely needed quality so difficult to acquire? And isn't it interesting that golf, like life itself, reveals this so clearly?

SWING THOUGHT

Do you need to pause for a while
and do some serious reflecting today?
Are you willing to slow down
long enough to ask God to direct
you in developing patience?

*P*ERHAPS THE STRONGEST INGREDIENT IN
THE MAKEUP OF A CHAMPION IS PATIENCE.

BYRON NELSON

Our Relationships

Part Eleven

Our Family Is Job #1
Ephesians 5:25; Luke 1:17

KEY VERSE

Husbands, love your wives, as Christ loved the church and gave himself up for her. . . . (Eph. 5:25)
He will go before him in the spirit and power of Elijah,
to turn the hearts of the fathers to the children. . . . (Luke 1:17)

In an interview with a Twin Cities reporter, Tom Lehman described how he has enjoyed steady progress toward success in his career. His career has been extremely important to him. Tom said that what matters to him is not so much to win a certain tournament or award but to be recognized and respected as one of a group of elite players.

What really matters to Tom, however, is something beyond the golf course. It is even beyond becoming someone who is recognized as an elite player. What really matters to Tom is what kind of a father and husband he has been and will be.

There are challenges to every husband and father, but Tom says the unique challenges as a tour golfer have to do with finding a routine that gives his wife and their three children the kind of time and attention they need and deserve. Being successful at golf actually makes it more difficult because

people expect so much of his time. There is no way he can meet everyone's expectations.

Tom believes our primary job on earth is to be the kind of husband and father God wants us to be. If we fail at this number one job, it doesn't matter how we perform in golf or in our work. We need to make certain that nothing, not even career success, gets in the way of being a godly father. We have no excuses, including the excuses of working hard to provide for our family or spending time to serve God.

SWING THOUGHT

*What are your godly
family responsibilities?
Have you allowed fame, career,
success, or time to get in the way of
those responsibilities? If so, today is
a good day to gain a fresh perspective
on what is truly important.*

The Encouragement of Friends
Hebrews 10:23–25

KEY VERSE

Let us consider how to stir up one another to love and good works, not neglecting to meet one another, as is the habit of some, but encouraging one another. (Heb. 10:24–25)

Nothing soothes the soul like the encouragement of understanding friends. Isn't it great to have one or two people who seem to understand your thoughts and feelings—even when you can't quite put them into words? These kinds of friends always seem to respond with the right words.

When we're experiencing pain or disappointment, they seem to know how to tell us that they understand and care. Just as important, when we have great joy or excitement, they are willing to share our exuberance and to encourage us. They also know when to say nothing.

SWING THOUGHT

We need to be givers and receivers of encouragement in our home, to our friends on the golf course, and to people in the rest of our life. With God's help, we can improve both in giving and receiving encouragement.

God is also our understanding friend. He is there to share our ups and our downs. Because Jesus has experienced the joys and pains of our human existence, he knows how to care deeply about our own emotions, both the ups and the downs. We are also blessed when God grants us the gift of friends who are able to encourage us in times of need and in times of joy.

We enjoy playing golf with people who are able to share the excitement of a great shot or stroke of good fortune (like a hole in one we don't deserve). We also enjoy playing with people who know what to say (or not say) when we hit a poor shot or make a miserable putt. They also understand that in the game of golf bad things sometimes still happen, even when we execute well.

Been There! Done That!
2 Corinthians 1:3–7

KEY VERSE

Who comforts us in all our affliction, so that we may be able to comfort those who are in any affliction, with the comfort with which we ourselves are comforted by God. (2 Cor. 1:4)

"Been there! Done that!" is a slang phrase. There is an expanded version: "Been there; done that; bought the tee shirt; read the book." Boasting like this means you're *very* familiar with the experience. While this slang phrase is lighthearted, the Scripture for today is similar—but extremely serious. It says that Jesus comforts us when we have afflictions, and we are to comfort others in similar situations.

What are these afflictions? They include all kinds of sickness, accidents, natural disasters, financial problems, etc. They are the things that cause us physical and emotional pain. It is the friend who has just learned he has cancer, the couple who loses a child in a bizarre accident, or someone who has recently lost his job.

Often those who are best at comforting others are those who have dealt with afflictions in their own life. But ultimately it is the "God of all comfort"

who gives us the love and mercy to share with others.

Greg Norman took out a full page in *Golf World* to thank those who had expressed encouragement following his dramatic slide in the 1996 Masters. Pros and amateurs alike are able to offer solace and encouragement to a fellow golfer. It is common to see tour professionals helping one another make an improvement. This may occur moments after they were doing their best to outplay one another for thousands of dollars and the rewards of winning a tournament. They know the feeling of having been there and having done that.

SWING THOUGHT

Having "been there and done that" may be your golden opportunity to give a word of comfort to someone who is currently experiencing some "affliction" on the golf course or in the game of life.

*P*UTTING IS
LIKE WISDOM,
PARTLY A
NATURAL GIFT
AND PARTLY THE
ACCUMULATION
OF EXPERIENCE.

Arnold Palmer

Hospitality to Strangers
Hebrews 13:1–3

--- KEY VERSE ---

Do not neglect to show hospitality to strangers,
for thereby some have entertained angels unawares. (Heb. 13:2)

At a golf course there are opportunities to show hospitality to strangers every day. We walk by new people, meet members of the staff as they serve the public, and may be paired with someone we have never met. If we do not have our own foursome, then we may meet one to three other people. When playing in an event we may be paired with other individuals we have not known before.

Scripture is clear when it says, "Do not neglect to show hospitality to strangers, for thereby some have entertained angels unawares." In Matthew 24 Jesus says, *"whenever you did this to the least of these you did it to me."*

We are clearly encouraged to show hospitality. It is quite common to find golfers showing great kindness to one another. At most golf courses a stranger is welcomed into a foursome. People tend to show politeness to one another on the course, both those within their foursome and to other groups. Unfortunately, however, this is not always the case, and arguments can quickly occur over pace of play, rule infractions, and other misunderstandings.

The goal for hospitality to strangers is not only to eliminate negative actions but to increase the positive behavior. We are to show hospitality to strangers. That means we are to see them as Christ would see them. We are to represent ourselves as proper ambassadors for Christ and to treat strangers as we would treat Christ himself if he were playing with us.

SWING THOUGHT

Hospitality is a matter of the heart that is revealed in our actions and in our words. Hospitality to strangers is an expectation Christ has given to us.

Iron Sharpens Iron
Proverbs 27:17

KEY VERSE

Iron sharpens iron, and one man sharpens another. (Prov. 27:17)

For most of us, the greatest golfing partners are those who are fun to be around—people who just enjoy the game. It's great when they are close in handicap, like to talk about the same things, are equally competitive, and—this is a great plus—are available to go and play *when and where we like to play.*

Another desirable quality for serious golfers is someone who helps them sharpen their game. By playing with this person we become better golfers over time; it seems we always play our best golf with that person. These are people who know the game of golf, know us, and know our game. They're willing to make a comment at an appropriate time to help us improve. Often it's on the practice tee, after the round, or even during the round itself. It's comments like, "You're not finishing as high as you usually do"; "You went past parallel that time"; "Try hitting about two inches behind the ball on that type of sand shot."

In the passage of Scripture above, the psalmist is referring to this kind of person. We all need people who are willing to help shape and sharpen us. People who will keep giving us feedback, who are willing to make helpful comments and will be enough of a friend to confront us with reality—and truth—whenever necessary.

SWING THOUGHT

*We need to be "iron" to one another
and allow others to be "iron"
for us so we may be shaped and
sharpened throughout life.
Who is "iron" to you?
Who is friend enough to
speak the truth to you in love?*

The Body of Christ—A Bag of Clubs
1 Corinthians 12:4–30

KEY VERSE

*For just as the body is one and has many members, and all the members of the body, though
many, are one body, so it is with Christ. For by one Spirit we were all baptized into one body—
Jews or Greeks, slave or free—and all were made to drink of one Spirit.* (1 Cor. 12:12–13)

The Body of Christ is that collection of people who have established a relationship with him. As such, they are a gallery of unique individuals with differing talents, gifts, and capabilities. In Scripture, this Body is likened to the body of a person. All parts of the body of a person are needed for effective functioning. None is more important than the other. The eye does not say to the hand that it is not needed, or vice versa. While the body may learn to function without some of its parts, it is not going to move at full capacity, and it will not function as well. Even a stubbed toe can slow us down.

A bag of golf clubs is a lot like the body of a person or the Body of Christ. Each club in the bag has a special function. While it is possible to play without one of the woods, irons, or even the putter, it is limiting for success and pleasure. For example, when a player accidentally or intentionally breaks a putter that person must find a way to finish the round using some other club. Most of us have not even tried putting with a wedge, driver, or two-iron, let alone finishing a tournament round of golf in that predicament. It's quite an experience.

Again, it's a great analogy to how the Body of Christ functions. The good news is that God has created us uniquely for his purpose. As we learn to use—and respect—the critical differences of the clubs in our bag, we also must learn to respect the uniqueness of those individuals around us. We are even to encourage one another in the use of our unique talents and gifts.

SWING THOUGHT

Play a round of golf without your putter to see what it's like. It should be quite an experience. Then identify one or more people you know in the Body of Christ who are truly different from you. Can you learn to love them and respect these individuals?

I PLAY FOR FUN,
FRIENDS, EXERCISE,
AND FRESH AIR.

BILL ROLAND

Keep on Going to the Finish

Part Twelve

Press on Toward the Mark
Philippians 3:12–16

---- KEY VERSE ----

I press on toward the goal for the prize of the upward call of God in Christ Jesus.
(Phil. 3:14)

P aul reminds the Christians at Philippi that even he must continue to strive toward the mark of perfection in his walk with Jesus. He is referring to the goal of "the surpassing worth of knowing Christ Jesus my Lord."

He says he seeks to "know him and the power of his resurrection, . . . share his sufferings, becoming like him in death." Once we have acknowledged Jesus as the Son of God and have accepted him as our Savior and Lord, then we, too, should "press on toward the mark." As Paul says, we must strive to press on toward the mark of achieving greater closeness with the Lord Jesus Christ. We do not do this for self-gain or for our own pride but for the joy of the process itself, and to become more like Jesus.

It is clear that even with God's help we will never achieve perfection in this process. We can only hold on to that which we have attained (verse 16) and continue "straining forward to what lies ahead" (verse 13).

The parallel to golf is incredible. No serious students of the game would suggest they have already, or could ever, achieve perfection. But, we still press on toward the mark of achieving that level of skill that is within our reach.

Some people strive to improve through lessons, practice, training devices, video, magazine subscriptions, and by playing as much as possible. While it may seem trivial compared to the high calling of our relationship with Jesus Christ, this analogy gives us some idea of the meaning of the passage.

SWING THOUGHT

Though perfection is unattainable, we still press on toward that mark. In your desire to be the best, never forget that you have an even higher calling—to give God your best today and always.

You can tell a lot about a person,
even a total stranger, by playing
a round of golf with him.

JOHN FREEMAN

Live One Step at a Time
Matthew 6:33

KEY VERSE

But seek first his kingdom and his righteousness, and all these things shall be yours as well.
(Matt. 6:33)

God wants us to take our thoughts and plans before him. In fact, he wants us to first seek him in all things. Still, how often we move out ahead of him with our thoughts and actions.

Can you recall a time in golf when you got ahead of where you should have been focused? Perhaps you were on the green with the chance to make a birdie putt, but you missed it because you were thinking about the water on the next tee shot. It is too easy to look three or four steps ahead in golf or in life.

Who hasn't been blocked by a tree and had to chip or punch out into

the open. In that situation, we need to learn to play the current shot so that it allows us to move forward once we get out of trouble. We must be careful not to leap ahead. That might cause us to lose concentration for the task at hand.

We play golf much better when we take one step at a time. We need to stop and assess our present situation on each shot. Relax and enjoy the shot and the hole without anticipating or worrying about what lies ahead.

In winning the 1996 U. S. Open, Steve Jones gave credit to learning this lesson from Ben Hogan's book *Hogan*. Steve's summary was, "Focus in on each shot and don't worry about the outcome."

SWING THOUGHT

"Focus in on each shot and don't worry about the outcome." Keep your mind on one thing at a time. When you do this, the rest usually will take care of itself.

Finish the Race—Keep the Faith
2 Timothy 4:6–8

KEY VERSE

I have fought the good fight, I have finished the race,
I have kept the faith. (2 Tim. 4:7)

Patty Berg, one of the early, great female professionals on the Ladies Professional Golf Tour is said to have offered this golf tip:

Finish high and you watch them fly.

Finish low and you watch them roll.

Swing to the finish and hold.

The simplicity of these three statements increases their value. Especially since not finishing the swing is such a common problem.

It's the same in life. Many people start, but fail to follow through to the finish. It may be a project at home or a task at work. It may be a good idea, but most jobs never make it to the finish line.

In this passage, Paul is writing to his young friend Timothy and is expressing his own sense of satisfaction as he approaches the end of his life. He says, I have:

Fought the good fight

Finished the race

Kept the faith

In other words, Paul is saying, "I have done my best in every situation; I did not give up before the end; and all along the way I have kept the faith in Christ which has sustained me."

Had Paul been a golfer, he might have said, "I struggled to make pars and bogies; I held together through the round; never once did I falter from my game plan to serve Jesus. I stayed 'in his grip.' Praise be to God!" Will you do the same?

SWING THOUGHT

Will you stay "in his grip"?
We pray you will.

About the Authors

JIM SHEARD holds a Ph.D. in organizational behavior and has been an executive and consultant for over 25 years. He now devotes his time to writing and speaking. Jim is an amateur golfer with a handicap in the mid-teens, and he is filled with determination to improve!

Jim Sheard awaits a tee time at Town & Country Golf Club

WALLY ARMSTRONG first recognized his need for a relationship with Christ during his graduate work at the University of Florida. While serving as a caddie for such legendary figures as Gary Player, Wally heard Billy Graham use analogies from golf to teach spiritual truths from the Bible.

Wally blasts out of a sand trap at Alaqua Country Club

Wally competed in over 300 PGA Tour events worldwide, gaining a lifetime membership to the PGA Tour. In his first Masters Tournament, Wally finished just three strokes behind Gary Player, setting a record rookie score of 280. As a golf instructor, Wally adopted part of the same teaching style he had learned from Dr. Graham and has put this to use in his own videos, clinics and books on golf.

Wally typically signs his name using the phrase, "In His grip." Golf brought Jim and Wally together—their desire to live *in His grip* has become their greatest bond.

PLEASE CONTACT US FOR INFORMATION ON:

—Ordering study guides for *In His Grip*
—Starting a golf fellowship/study group
—Hosting a golf event or clinic
—Subscribing to our newsletter

In His Grip Resources
P. O. Box 642
Owatonna, MN 55060-0642.

1(888)899-GRIP(4747)
1(507)455-3377

THE GOOD SHOTS KEEP US COMING BACK.

JOHN FREEMAN